Viva CHE!

VIVA CHE!

The Strange Death and Life of
CHE GUEVARA

ANDREW SINCLAIR

SUTTON PUBLISHING

This book was first published by
Lorrimer Publishing Limited, © 1968

This new revised edition first published in 2006 by
Sutton Publishing Limited · Phoenix Mill
Thrupp · Stroud · Gloucestershire · GL5 2BU

British Library Cataloguing in Publication Data
A catalogue record for this book is available from the British Library.

ISBN 0 7509 4310 6

Typeset in 12/14pt Photina.
Typesetting and origination by
Sutton Publishing Limited.
Printed and bound in Great Britain by
J.H. Haynes & Co. Ltd, Sparkford.

Contents

Acknowledgements

We are especially grateful to the following people who contributed much time and effort to the project: Denise Alexandre, Jorge Bolaños, Alberto Korda, Osvaldo Salas and Cecil Woolf.

We would like to thank, for their help and suggestions, Téofilo Acosta, Ana Ortega Cáceres, Marysa Gerassi, Luis Korda, Verney Leech, Derek Lindsay, Ellen Maslow, Rafael Morante, Roberto Fernández Retamar, Guido Sanchez, Marie Schébéko, Daniel Schechter, Raúl Lazo Sotolongo, Jorge Timossi and Ed Victor.

Our thanks are also due to Casa de las Américas, the Cuban Embassy in London, Comision para perpetuar la memoria del Comandante Ernesto Guevara, Revista Cuba and Departamento de Prensa Extrangera (Ministerio de Relaciones Exteriores).

We would also like to thank, for the use of their photographs, Studio Korda, Keystone Agency, Magnum (John Hill in London), Osvaldo Salas, Comision Orientacíon Revoluclonara and United Press International.

The piece by John Berger is reprinted by kind permission of *New Society*; the poem by Adrian Mitchell is reprinted by kind permission of *Peace News*; the piece by *OZ Magazine* is reprinted by kind permission of the editors; the song by Alasdair Clayre is included by kind permission of Albermarle Music, Ltd.

Other people have kindly helped us in many ways too various to specify. To all of these, our grateful thanks. Finally, we wish to thank all those who wrote in or sent contributions that we were unable to publish for lack of space.

Masa

At the end of the battle, when the fighter was dead,
A man came up to him and said:
'Do not die. I love you so.'
But, alas, the body stayed dead.

Two men came near him and repeated:
'Don't leave us. Be brave. Come back.'
But, alas, the body stayed dead.

Then twenty, a hundred, a thousand,
Five hundred thousand came and begged,
'Can so much love do nothing against death?'
But, alas, the body stayed dead.

Then millions came up; he was surrounded.
And all of them called: 'Brother, don't leave us. . . .'
But, alas, the body stayed dead.

Then all the men on earth came round.
The sad body saw them and was moved;
Slowly, he rose and kissed the first one,
And then began to walk. . . .

CÉSAR VALLEJO (Peru)
(1895–1939)

Notes on the Life of
Ernesto 'Che' Guevara

Ernesto Guevara de la Serna was born in Rosario, Argentina, on 14 June, 1928. His parents were Ernesto Guevara Lynch, civil engineer of Irish descent, and Celia de la Serna, of Spanish descent. This was a middle-class family with strong left-wing and liberal tendencies. The Guevaras were free-thinkers, admirers of José Martí, and on the side of the Republicans during the Spanish Civil War.

Ernesto was the eldest of five children; after him came Celia, Roberto, Ana Maria and Juan Martin, in that order.

JOSE AGUILAR: In 1937, my family fled from Spain to Argentina where, at Alta Gracia, a city in the province of Córdoba, we met the Guevaras. All the children became friends and played together every day, really almost living together. The Guevara children were very brave at games and sports, and we were a bit frightened of them. Ernesto like rough games very much; I remember one of his brothers, Roberto, telling me how Ernesto would jump across three feet of space from the third floor of their house to the next, just for kicks, and then make fun of the other chileren because they did not dare do the same thing.

In those days, our favourite writers were Jules Verne and Alexandre Dumas.

Later, when Ernesto started high school in the city of Córdoba, he studied English; but he always liked French better. He studied French with his mother and liked to read French poetry. He was also extremely fond of Pablo Neruda's poems, and would spend days reciting some of them aloud.

My father, who was a doctor, was upset by the fact that Ernesto read the works of Freud at the age of fourteen and that his parents did not mind.

FERNANDO BARRAL: I met Ernesto in 1940. He was already incredibly sure of himself and totally independent in his opinions. He was very dynamic, restless, and unconventional. I think I secretly

Che Guevara with his parents, Celia de la Serna and Ernesto Guevara Lynch.

envied him for his energy, his self-confidence and his boldness; the most striking thing about him was his absolute fearlessness. The way he played rugby also impressed us, and what made him so different from the rest of us was that he seemed much more 'tough'.

ALBERTO GRANADOS: I met Ernesto in 1941 when he was at high school with my brother Thomas. I was at University at the time. We Córdoba students, along with students from other universities, had gone on strike against the abuses committed on the university campuses. That was the reason I was arrested and taken to Córdoba central police commissariat. Rather than arrested, I should say kidnapped, for we were not tried. At that time my brother Thomas used to bring me food in jail, as they didn't feed us. One day, Ernesto, his school friend, came along. I spoke with the two of them and explained that the high school students should demonstrate in the streets so that people would know how we were being treated. What amazed me was young Ernesto Guevara's reaction to my proposal. He answered, 'Nothing doing, Alberto. Go out onto the streets so that the police can hit us with their clubs? Nothing doing. I'll go and demonstrate only if you give me a gun.'

CHE: At fifteen, a man already knows what he wants to die for, and he is not afraid of giving his life, if he has found an ideal which makes this sacrifice easy.

ALBERTO GRANADOS: In spite of the asthma he suffered from all his life, Ernesto was a sports enthusiast, something we had in common; an education which alternated between Baudelaire's poetry and sports forged him spiritually and made him physically fit. From then on, he became involved with travel and action. He was at high school and I was at university; but as he enjoyed our company and as we were impressed by his intelligence and the depth of his knowledge, we became great friends. I used his father's library a lot. Ernesto was the main reader, and I came second. Without a doubt, he had an intellectual sense which, from childhood, enabled him to distinguish himself in all aspects of life. He enjoyed going out with us on trips to the country, learning many things that were later useful to us on our motorcycle trip across the continent. Years later, those experiences were necessary to him as a guerrilla. He learned how to set up a tent with few resources. We learned all of those things without ever thinking of future possibilities: it was just a healthy outdoor way of life that allowed us to get away a little from the ordinary routine of the student and city-dweller.

In 1946 Ernesto Guevara finished high school and the Guevara family moved to Buenos Aires. There, Ernesto began his medical studies.

ALBERTO GRANADOS: We all thought that, because of his knowledge of and facility in mathematics, he would study engineering. We were surprised when he told us he had enrolled in medical school. He had a part-time job in the city government and also did some voluntary work in an institute for Allergy Research.

When Ernesto was eighteen years old, he registered for compulsory military service, in accordance with Argentinian law. He was examined by a board of military doctors who, because of his asthma, pronounced him unfit for military service of any sort.

During all his holidays, Ernesto would travel by whatever form of transport was available to him. He sometimes went on foot, and at other times used a bicycle which had a small motor on it. In this manner, he travelled round the various provinces of Argentina: Tucumán, Mendoza, Salta, Jujuy and La Rioja. On another occasion, he signed up as a crew member of a merchant marine ship and went to the Caribbean. It was his first trip abroad.

CHE: I must admit that I have never felt like a foreigner anywhere, neither in Cuba nor in any of the countries I have been to; I felt

Guatemalan in Guatemala, Mexican in Mexico, Peruvian in Peru. Just as I feel Cuban in Cuba today and, of course, Argentinian too, here and everywhere else.

ALBERTO GRANADOS: He used to say to his fellow students, 'While you stay here preparing for three exams, I plan to cover the province of Santa Fé, northern Córdoba, eastern Mendoza, and along the way, study to pass those courses right along with you.' And, of course, he did just that and maybe more. He covered the route he had planned and passed his courses on top of it. He wasn't concerned about his grades, he was more interested in studying what would be useful to him and not what was good for getting high marks. . . .

Touring Latin America, becoming acquainted with its beautiful sights and the misery in which its inhabitants lived, was a long cherished dream. On those nights that I spent in the company of Guevara and my brothers in some mountain zone on a weekend or an excursion, our conversation was full of our future trip.

On 29 December, 1951, Ernesto set off with Alberto Granados for a long trip across Latin America by motorcycle. They planned to visit the whole length of the Pacific coast.

ALBERTO GRANADOS: If the motorcycle had held up, the trip would certainly not have turned out to be such a valuable and rewarding personal experience as it did. But the risky motorcycle didn't make it. Shortly before we got to Santiago, Chile, when we still had not covered even an eighth part of our projected journey, the vehicle simply refused to go any further, and we mournfully wrapped it up in our pup-tent and left it in an out-of-the-way spot while we continued our voyage on foot. This change gave us an opportunity to know the people. We had to get various odd jobs to earn enough money to continue on our trip. We worked as truck drivers, porters, seamen, cops and doctors and dishwashers. Trudging along without a cent in our pockets, we arrived at the gates of the 'Braden Company' mine at Chuquicamata, Chile. Certainly, Braden and his cohorts never dreamed that in early 1952 the guard who was then sleeping in their sentry box with his feet resting on a pair of military boots was none other than the man who was later to make Yankee imperialism shiver in its boots: Major Ernesto Che Guevara.

The two young men reached Peru. They were appalled by the condition of the Indians, now totally degraded by hunger, exploitation and addiction to coca.

ALBERTO GRANADOS: I remember one day at Macchu Pichu where we stayed for several days. I was reclining on the 'sacrificial stone' among the ruins; Che was sitting next to me, preparing a hot drink. I was speaking about creating a workers' community in the Andes and then winning over the government to make a revolution for these poor people who receive so few of the benefits of civilization. Ernesto smiled and said, 'Make the revolution without firing a shot? Are you crazy?'

Guevara and Granados travelled by boat from the port of Pucalpa along the Ucayali River, which is a tributary of the Amazon. After a stay at Iquitos, they travelled on to San Pablo where they stayed at a leprosarium, working in the laboratory and living with the lepers, playing basketball with the patients, taking them on excursions and doing all they could to help.

When the time came to leave, Guevara and Granados decided to cross the Amazon and reach Leticia in Colombia, where the Amazon arrives at the intersection of three countries, Brazil, Peru and Colombia. The lepers built them a raft called the 'Mambo-Tango' and organised a going-away party for the two young doctors.

ALBERTO GRANADOS: There, despite a heavy drizzle, was a boat packed with patients: men, women and children. When we arrived they cheered us and immediately began to sing. Everyone else had already gathered there and the band was naturally there too, saxophone in the lead, carrying on a musical dialogue with the patients. Then came the speeches. First three of the patients spoke, simply, awkwardly, but affectionately, expressing admiration for our voyage. When the third patient finished, it was my turn to speak. I was very moved, so my speech was not very good. . . . When the applause ended, they sang a farewell song and began to leave slowly and silently. The most moving part of the ceremony was to see the white boat slowly slipping away in the mist and the rain while the song of the chorus still reached us. It seemed dreamlike; everything was embellished by the affection and sense of brotherhood that we all felt in that moment.

They had many adventures and difficulties, for they missed Leticia and drifted further down river. When they made their way back to Leticia, they worked as soccer coaches, then got arrested in Bogotá. Finally, they reached Venezuela. Granados decided to stay and work at a leprosarium in Caracas and Ernesto met a family friend who owned a plane for transporting race-horses. This plane was returning to Buenos Aires via Miami; so Ernesto set off for Miami.

ALBERTO GRANADOS: Che told us that he had a hard time in Miami, that he went a lot to the library, that at first he had only a cup of coffee and milk during the day, that he became friendly with the owner of a cafeteria who gave him some food - until one day a Puerto Rican came in and began talking against the Truman administration. He was overheard by an FBI agent, and it was the same old story. Che had to make himself scarce.

Ernesto finally got back to Buenos Aires and continued his studies. He received his MD in March, 1953.

JOSE AGUILAR: He finished his student's career in a meteoric fashion, not terribly well, without getting brilliant marks, but extremely fast.

CHE: When I began my medical studies, most of my ideals as a revolutionary did not exist. Like most other people, I longed for success. I dreamed of being a famous researcher and achieving something which might ultimately be of use to humanity. But due to a series of circumstances and also partly due to inclination, I began to travel all over America and got to know it well. Because of the conditions in which I travelled, I came into close contact with poverty and hunger and disease. Through lack of means, I discovered I was unable to cure sick children, and I saw the degradation of undernourishment and constant repression. In this way, I began to realise that there was another thing which was as important as being a famous researcher or making a great contribution to medical science: and that was to help those people.

JOSE AGUILAR: I noticed when he returned from that trip that he was much more interested in political issues. I heard him reading out a passage from his diary about Macchu Pichu. It was about the Spanish colonial domination which had taken over the Indian culture; he described the Catholic churches he had seen which had been built over and had incorporated Inca remains.

After his graduation, Ernesto set out for Venezuela to visit Granados. With two or three companions he took a milk train that went from Buenos Aires to La Paz, a six-thousand mile trip. The train stopped at every city, large or small. He then crossed Lake Titicaca and went down to the coast to get to Venezuela. When he reached Guayaquil in Ecuador, he met Ricardo Rojo, an Argentinian lawyer in exile who had made a spectacular escape from prison, seeking asylum at the Guatemalan embassy in Buenos Aires. When Ernesto told Rojo that he was on his way to Caracas, Rojo replied: 'But Guevara, why do you want to go to Venezuela, a country that's good only for making money? Come with me to Guatemala where there's a real social revolution taking place.'
    Granados received a note from Ernesto a few days later. It said, 'Petiso, I'm going to Guatemala. I'll write to you later.'

Ernesto Guevara arrived in Guatemala on 24 December, 1953. This was the beginning of 'El Che'.' Because Argentinians use the monosyllable 'che' to punctuate their conversation, Central Americans call anyone who comes from Argentina by this name.

CHE: To me, 'Che' is the most important and most cherished part of my life. It means so much to me; everything that came before it, my surname and my Christian name, are minor, personal and insignificant details.

When Ernesto Guevara arrived in Guatemala, he wanted to go and practise as a doctor in the jungle. He made an application, but the Guatemalan authorities demanded that he renew his doctor's diploma first, which would have meant more years of study. Instead, he stayed in Guatemala City, leading a life on the margin of poverty, but full of social rewards. He met many young Latin American revolutionaries, including Hilda Gadea from Peru, who became his first wife.

The Moncada Barracks immediately after the 26 July attack.

DARIO LOPEZ: The first time I saw Che in Guatemala, he owned only one pair of worn-out shoes and always wore the same shirt that was never properly tucked into his trousers. I think he was heading for the hospital where he worked. Nico López pointed him out to me and said, 'Look, there's Che, the Argentine.' He was going through a very difficult period, and the only clothes he owned were the ones on his back. Occasionally, he would casually ask a pal, 'Could you lend me a pair of trousers or a shirt?' (At times, the trousers were too big, but he didn't seem to mind.)

Nico López belonged to a group of young Cuban exiles who had participated in the assault on the Moncada and the Bayamo fortresses in Santiago de Cuba on 26 July, 1953. This assault had failed, but it had led to the formation of Fidel Castro's '26 of July' movement and in his departure for Mexico after his imprisonment.

HILDA GADEA: Nico López used to tell us all about what Fidel Castro had done. He admired Fidel, and it was during that period that many of us Latin American exiles began to respect Fidel. Nico would describe Fidel's discretion, the spirit of sacrifice with which he and his followers had attacked the Moncada fortress. Nico not only admired Fidel, but also had tremendous faith in him.

In February, 1953, Jacobo Arbenz's left-wing régime had expropriated 225,000 uncultivated acres of arable land from the United Fruit Company owned by American investors.

Fidel Castro's plan of attack on the Moncada barracks.

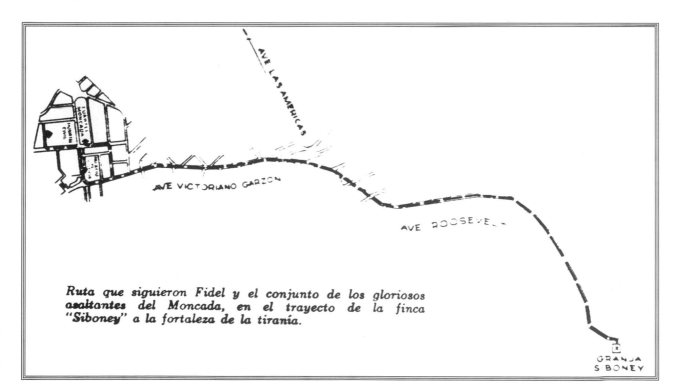

Ruta que siguieron Fidel y el conjunto de los gloriosos asaltantes del Moncada, en el trayecto de la finca "Siboney" a la fortaleza de la tiranía.

CHE: The last American revolutionary democracy – that of Jacobo Arbenz – still in power in this area failed as a result of the cold premeditated aggression carried out by the USA, hiding behind the smokescreen of its continental propaganda. Its visible head was the Secretary of State, Dulles, a man who, through a rare coincidence, was also a stockbroker and an attorney of the United Fruit Company. When the American invasion first took place, I tried to get together a group of young men like myself to fight back. In Guatemala, it was necessary to fight and almost nobody fought. It was necessary to resist, and almost nobody resisted.

HILDA GADEA: During the aggression, Che volunteered for guard duty while there was a black-out and the city was being bombed. He asked to go to the front, but he was never sent. Everyone knew he wanted to go and he finally had to take refuge in the Argentinian embassy. It was Guatemala, which finally convinced him of the necessity for armed struggle and for taking the initiative against imperialism. By the time he left, he was sure of this.

MARIO DALMAU: Che had read the complete works of Marx and Lenin, and a whole pantheon of Marxist thinkers. His views were very lucid although, like all Argentinians, he liked to argue about them.

CHE: At that time, when I was in Arbenz's Guatemala, I had begun taking notes to try and assess what would be the duties of a revolutionary doctor. Then, after the United Fruit Company aggression, I realised one fundamental thing: to be a revolutionary doctor, you needed a revolution first.

In the summer of 1954, I slipped out of Guatemala into Mexico. FBI agents were already arresting and killing off all those who might endanger the United Fruit Company government. In Mexico, I met up again with some militants of the 26 of July movement, whom I had known in Guatemala. I also became friendly with Raúl Castro, Fidel's brother, and it was he who introduced me to the leader of the movement.

FIDEL CASTRO: Che was one of those people, whom everybody liked on sight for his simplicity, his character, his naturalness, his sense of comradeship, his personality and his originality, even before finding out all the other fine qualities which distinguished him. His political formation had already attained a high degree of development. To convince a man of his type to join us did not need many arguments.

CHE: After my experiences travelling all over Latin America and after Guatemala, it would have taken very little to persuade me to join any revolution against a tyranny; but Fidel made a very great impression on me. He would confront the most impossible situations and resolve them. He was absolutely positive that if we set off for Cuba, we would get there. That once we got there, we would fight, and that by fighting, we would win. His optimism was contagious. We had to act, to fight, so consolidate our position. To stop moaning and to start the real struggle. And in order to prove to the Cuban people that they could trust his word, he made his famous speech, 'In 1956, we shall be free men or martyrs', announcing that, before the year was over, he would land somewhere in Cuba at the head of an expeditionary force.

Che began to train for guerrilla warfare in Mexico with the other young men who had decided to follow Fidel back to Cuba.

CHE: My almost immediate impression after attending the first few classes was that victory was possible, something I had doubted when I joined the rebel chief.

On 25 November, 1956, the small yacht 'Granma' set off for Cuba, with eighty-three men aboard. Their object was to liberate Cuba from the military dictatorship of Fulgencio Batista.
After a terrible journey, during which all the men aboard the 'Granma' were racked with sea-sickness, they finally landed in Cuba, near Belic, a province of Oriente, and tried to head towards the Sierra Maestra mountain chain. Through inexperience, they got bogged down in a swamp and, after they emerged, they camped in a highly unsuitable spot in the sugar-cane fields. This place was known as Alegría de Pío.

MAJOR FAUSTINO PEREZ: At the mention of Alegría de Pío, the first thing that comes to my mind is the doctor who came with the 'Granma' expedition. I'm thinking of Che in the grip of an asthma attack that never let up, while he never uttered a word of complaint. When we stopped to rest at Alegría de Pío, at a time when all of us, even the ones in perfect health, felt completely exhausted, Che devoted almost the entire day to caring for comrades, whose feet had been cut to ribbons by the long walk.

But Fidel and his men had been spotted by Batista's army, which had closed on the unsuspecting men and was now ready to attack.

CHE: At four o'clock that afternoon, without the slightest warning and to our complete surprise, we heard a shot, followed by a symphony of lead over our heads. In the kaleidoscopic scene, men ran by shouting, the wounded called for help, some men tried to take

Che Guevara riding in the Sierra Maestra.

cover behind slender stalks of sugar-cane as if they were tree trunks, while others signalled in terror for silence by placing a finger over their lips amidst the roar of battle. . . . I personally felt the unpleasant sensation in my flesh of a simultaneous baptism of fire and blood. We got out of there as best we could, every man for himself or in groups, not heeding our leader's orders, without contact with our captains and in a state of complete confusion. I remember the push that Major Almeida gave me since I did not wish to walk, and it was only thanks to his imperious orders that I got up and kept going, believing all the time that I was near death.

Of the eighty-two men who had set out with Fidel, only fifteen were left after the Alegría de Pío disaster. These fifteen wandered about in scattered groups through the cane-fields for nine days before finally meeting up again with their leader, Fidel.

When Fidel, who had only two men with him, joined up with the other twelve survivors of the 'Granma' expedition, he made his shortest speech: 'We have already won the war.'

CHE: It was incredible that this small group of men who did not know each other very well already spoke of victory and taking the initiative. But the one who had the greatest faith in the people, who at all times showed his extraordinary powers of leadership, was Fidel. Already, during those nights sitting under the trees anywhere, those long nights since our activities ceased at nightfall, we began to draw plan after plan for the present, for the near future, and for victory. The days passed, and, little by little, new recruits came in. The first peasants started joining us, some unarmed, some with weapons that had been left by our comrades in the homes of friendly people, or abandoned in the cane-fields as they fled.

FIDEL CASTRO: Then came our first victory and Che was already a soldier by then, as well as our doctor.

CHE: Our small troop already had twenty-two rifles at the time we stormed La Plata on 17 January, 1957, forty-five days after our landing. We caught an Army Post of twelve to fifteen men by surprise, and they surrendered after an hour of fighting. Thus twelve new rifles were obtained from this action.

FIDEL CASTRO: By the time we had a second victory at El Uvero, May, 1957, Che was not only a soldier, but *the* most outstanding of that battle. He performed for the first time those amazing feats which became typical of everything he did.

Opposite: Che Guevara with Fidel Castro.

Fidel Castro and Che Guevara during their guerrilla campaign in the Sierra Maestra.

CHE: The battle for the military detachment of El Uvero was the fiercest of the war; of the 120 to 140 men who took part, forty were put out of action, which meant that the dead and wounded amounted to approximately thirty per cent of the total combatants. The political outcome of the battle was extraordinary because it took place in one of the few moments – after the 'Granma' invasion – when there was no press censorship in the island. The whole of Cuba spoke about El Uvero.

FIDEL CASTRO: On this occasion, Che distinguished himself, not only as a fighter, but as a doctor, helping both his wounded comrades and the enemy soldiers. As we had to leave El Uvero, hunted down by fresh enemy troops, someone had to stay behind with the wounded, and so Che remained. Helped by a small group of soldiers, he hid them, looked after them, saved their lives, and with them eventually joined up with our column once more.

CHE: In the early nomadic phase of guerrilla warfare, the guerrilla doctor must go everywhere with his comrades and fulfil all the other duties of a guerrilla as well, including that of combat. He must undertake the exhausting and sometimes heartbreaking task of looking after sick men without having in his possession the medicine

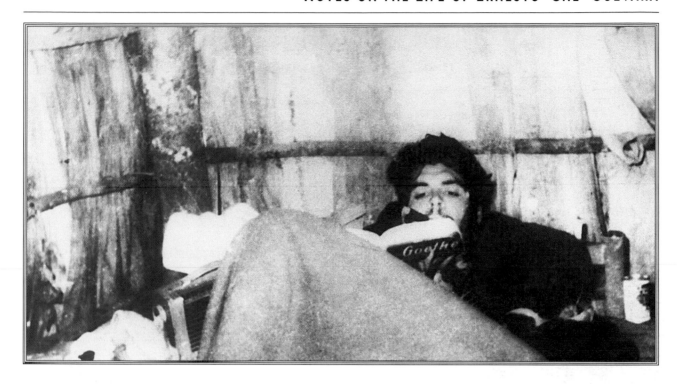

that would enable him to save a man's life. During this stage, the doctor has the most influence on the other men and their morale, because, to a man in pain, a simple aspirin takes on importance, if it is administered by someone who identifies with his suffering. During this phase, the doctor must identify completely with the ideals of the revolution, for his words will have more impact on the men than anybody else's.

When he returned with his little band of wounded to Fidel's column in July, 1957, Che was made leader of the second column to be formed in the Sierra Maestra.

CHE: A new column was being organised, with me as Captain. The column was made up of some thirty-five men, variously dressed and variously armed, but I was very proud of them. A few nights later, I was to feel still prouder and closer to the Revolution, if that was possible, still more desirous of proving that my officer's insignia was deserved. We were writing a letter of greetings and appreciation to 'Carlos' – Frank País's clandestine name – which was signed by all the officers of the guerrilla army who knew how to write – many of the Sierra peasants did not know how to read or write, but they were part of the guerrillas. The signatures appeared in one column and, next to them in another column, the signer's rank. When my turn came to sign, Fidel said simply, 'Make it Major.' Thus, informally and almost off-handedly, I was promoted to Major of the Second Column of the

Che Guevara reading Goethe in the guerrilla camp of 'El Hombrito' in the Sierra Maestra.

Guerrilla Army, later known as Column No. 4. The trace of vanity that is within all of us made me feel the proudest man in the world that day. The symbol of my new rank, a small star, was given to me by Celia, together with one of the wrist-watches that had been ordered from Manzanillo. From that time on, we in the Second Column, much less harassed than the First headed by Fidel because of our lesser political importance, were able to form the bases of the first factories and more permanent camps, which would end our nomadic life. We carried through some actions of little importance, but the most important thing was precisely that stabilisation, worked out with great difficulty by transporting materials from very distant regions on our shoulders.

RAFAEL CHAO: His black beret had a tiny gilt metal star on it. He could be seen, sometimes very late, sitting on his hammock and writing down his notes. He never took a rest without writing down some notes. He also liked discussion very much. When everyone was already asleep, he would take a walk through the camp, looking for someone who felt like having a talk.

ONIRIA GUTIERREZ, *the first woman member of Che's column, who joined up in August, 1957, when she was only eighteen*: On one occasion Che asked me about my religious beliefs. This led me to ask him if he himself was religious. 'No,' he answered, 'I can't be religous because I'm a communist.' I was dumbfounded; being so young, I had had no political education and had only ever been told terrible things about communists. So that I jumped up in my hammock and protested, 'No, you can't be a communist because you're such a good man.' This made Che laugh a great deal and he began explaining to me all the things I did not know.

On another occasion, we sat discussing in a group. There were some among us who always used to say that, once we had won against Batista, we would have to go and fight in other countries; it was while we were discussing this that I asked Che, 'Do you feel Argentinian, Che? How did you come to be here? I can understand why we're here, but you . . .' He understood what I meant and answered me with his usual kindness. I will never forget what he said, 'It's because we all have to help one another.' I also remember him saying that he would not die of old age; he insisted on this point because, even then, I think he always meant to go on with the struggle.

CHE: We were able to put up a shoe factory and a saddlery, an armoury with its electric lathe, a tin works, and a smithy for the purpose, among other things, of filling small metal grenades to be fired from a gun – an invention of ours. It was fired with a blank

Opposite: Che Guevara carries a litter during the Sierra Maestra campaign.

Fidel Castro and Che Guevara in the Sierra Maestra.

23

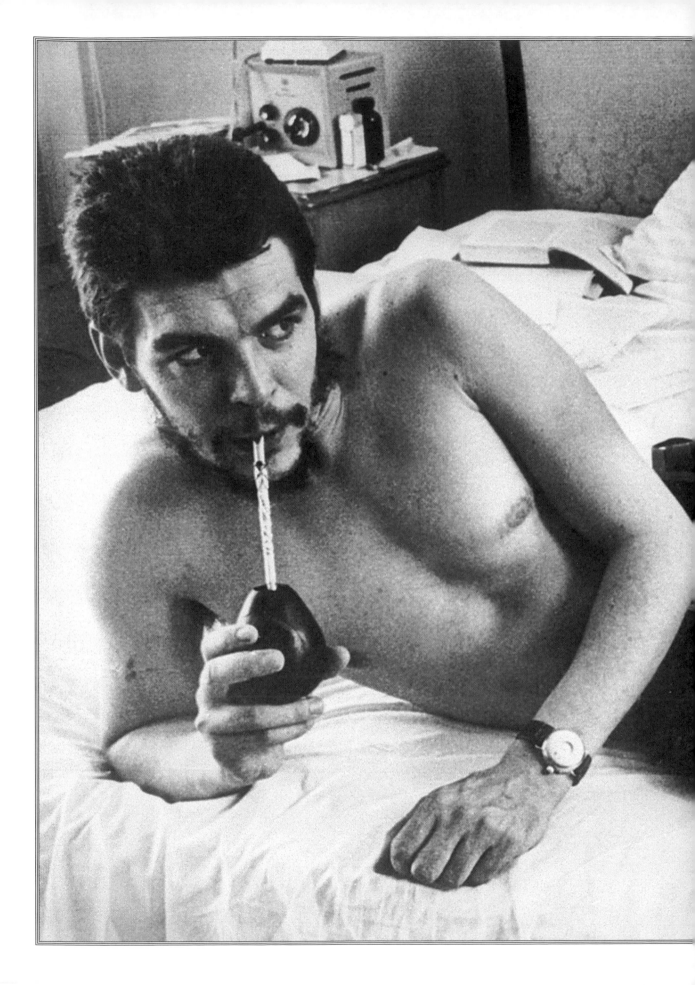

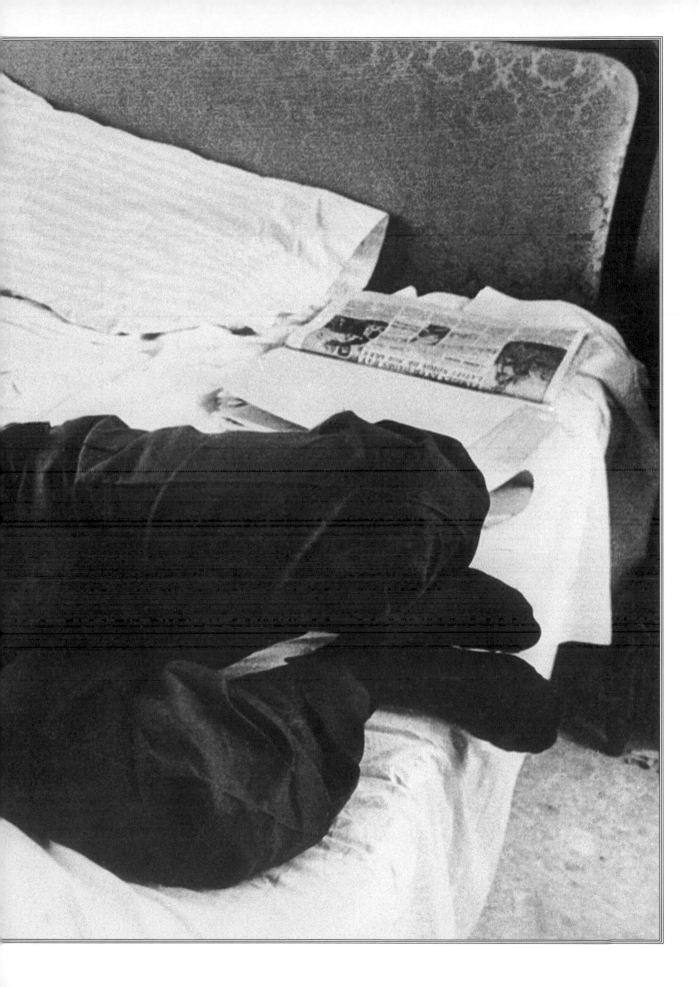

cartridge and was dubbed 'M-26'. We also built schools, recreation areas and ovens to bake bread. Later on, the Radio Rebelde transmitter was installed, and our first clandestine newspaper *El Cubano Libre* was published.

RICARDO MARTINEZ, *an announcer for Radio Rebelde*: I remember that Comandante Ernesto Che Guevara used to smoke a pipe on which were carved the names of places where he had fought. The pipe was covered with Sierra Maestra names, Alegría de Pío, La Plata, Palma Mocha, El Uvero, El Hombrito, Pino del Agua. . . .

El Che always drank *maté*, which is an Argentinian custom, and he took coffee without sugar. He carried a camera about with him, along with the gun which never left his side, and the equally vital inhaler which he used to overcome his attacks of asthma.

Often, he used to go about riding on a white mule.

On one occasion, when the Argentinian journalist, Jorge Ricardo Masetti, interviewed him on the Conrado Heights near the rebel radio station, enemy planes began to drop bombs on the area.

Instinctively, everyone dived for cover under the trees except for Che who refused to move. He insisted on continuing the interview with Masetti while the bombardment was going on. His reason was that the sound of gunfire and of bombs exploding, which would be heard over the broadcast, would prove to listeners that the criminal dictatorship cared nothing for the lives of the peasants in the area.

It was a bold reaction and we all felt ashamed of having taken cover; and so we left our hiding places and followed the example of Comandante Guevara who still sat there calmly carrying on with the interview.

A whole succession of victories now began for the guerrilla army which had effectively liberated a part of Cuban territory. In one victorious battle after another against Batista's army, the guerrillas were able to capture more and more arms, also recruiting more and more men, both from the cities and the countryside. In March, 1958, Major Raúl Castro, at the head of the Sixth Column, was able to go and form a Second Eastern Front in the north of the Oriente Province. By the summer of 1958, the guerrilla army felt strong enough to start moving west up the island towards Havana.

CHE: It was decided to initiate a march to Las Villas, the central province of Cuba. In the military order sent to us, the principal strategic plan indicated was to cut systematically the communications between the two extremities of the island. Further, I was ordered to establish relations with all the political groups that were in the mountain parts of that region and was given ample military powers to govern the zone under my charge.

It turned out to be an extremely difficult and arduous undertaking. Che's column had to march through unprotected and unfriendly territory, constantly harassed by Batista's army, without the cover of the Sierra hills nor the support of the Oriente population.

Che Guevara just after the guerrillas entered Havana in January, 1959.

CHE: Those were the days of fatiguing marches across desolate areas with nothing but mud and water. We were hungry, we were thirsty, and we could hardly move ahead; our legs felt like lead, and our weapons weighed us down. A mood of pessimism came creeping in. Hunger and thirst, fatigue, a feeling of helplessness in the face of the enemy, which was encircling us more and more, and above all, the terrible foot disease known in the country as *mazamorra* – which made each step taken by our soldiers intolerable torture – turned us into an army of ghosts. Day by day, the physical condition of our troop was deteriorating. We had food every other day, and not always then. The only way to keep the exhausted men going was by swearing at them, pleading with them, and yelling insults at them.

After a month and a half of marching, the exhausted troop finally reached the mountain range of Las Villas, 'that blue patch in the West' which filled Che's men with new hope when they first saw it in the distance.

CHE: Our first job when we arrived in the Sierra del Escambray was clearly defined: to harass the dictatorship's military apparatus, above all his communications. Our immediate objective was to prevent elections from being held. But work was made difficult by the short time left before the elections, which were scheduled for 3 November. The days preceding were ones of extraordinary activity: our columns mobilised in all directions, with the result that few voters in those areas cast ballots. Troops led by Camilo Cienfuegos in the northern part of the province paralysed the electoral farce. In general, everything from the transport of Batista soldiers to the movement of merchandise came to a halt. In the November and December of 1958, we gradually closed off the highways. The central railway line was cut at several points. And so the island was effectively divided. Nearly all communications between Havana and the cities east of Santa Clara were cut off.

Che's column was able to take and to hold many towns on the way to Santa Clara, the principal objective. Fomento, Cabaiguan, Guaios and Placetas all fell. On 29 December, 1958, Che and his men attacked Santa Clara, the focal point of the island's central plain, a city with a population of 150,000, which was the nerve centre of the nation's railways and communications. In spite of an armoured train rushed by Batista's army to the city, Santa Clara fell. This last campaign, brilliantly planned and fought by Che, helped finally to overthrow Batista's regime. It was just after the fall of Santa Clara that Batista fled Cuba. On 2 January, 1959, Che Guevara and Camilo Cienfuegos entered Havana at the head of their columns.

CHE: I believe that the Cuban Revolution accomplished three radical alterations in the mechanism of Latin American revolutionary movements by demonstrating that:
1. The people's forces can win a war against the regular army.
2. It is not necessary to wait until all conditions are favourable to start a revolution; the insurrection itself can bring about those conditions.
3. In the underdeveloped nations of America, the basic field of action for armed struggle must be the countryside.

On 9 February, 1959, in consideration for services rendered to Cuba, Che Guevara was declared a full-fledged Cuban citizen by the Council of Ministers. On 2 June, he married his comrade-in-arms, Aleida March, whom he had met during the revolutionary war. A few days later, he left for an extended tour of the Afro-Asian countries. This was to be the first of many such tours of the countries of the Third World and the socialist nations. Che acted as a representative of the Cuban Revolution and as head of various Cuban commercial delegations and missions. In the October of

Opposite: Che Guevara during the campaign of Las Villas at the Rebel Radio Station in the Escambray.

Fidel Castro celebrates his victory in 1957.

Che Guevara at the time of the battle of Santa Clara; to the left is his comrade-in-arms, Aleida March, whom he married in June, 1959.

Che Guevara and other guerrillas at the end of the Cuban Revolution.

that year, he was made chief of the Industrial Department of the National Institute of Agrarian Reform.

CHE: Agrarian reform meant the destruction of monopolies which prevented the peasantry from working the land. It meant helping them to grow produce without the fear of getting into debt or being squeezed by the land-owners. From the start, the reform guaranteed to both farmers and agricultural workers the ownership of the land, the necessary technical aid of qualified personnel, and material and financial assistance. It eliminated the *latifundia* system which had consisted of paying rent with a part of the crop. It meant the full use and cultivation of arable lands which, under the capitalist-monopolistic system, had been deliberately allowed to remain fallow for economic reasons. It also tended towards the gradual elimination of the one-crop economics, sugar in the case of Cuba, which is the bane of underdeveloped countries.

On 26 November, 1959, the Council of Ministers appointed Che Guevara President of the National Bank of Cuba, in charge of the nation's finances. Many banknotes in Cuba still carry the signature: 'Che'.

Che Guevara experiments with scientific technology.

IVAN ARGENTINSKI: My second meeting was in his office, as Governor of the National Bank. A very comfortably furnished room, left over from the past. Che Guevara met me like an old friend and said that he was entirely at my disposal. I started with a story which I had just heard:

After the victory, Fidel Castro called his nearest assistants and said:

'I want one of us to be Governor of the National Bank. Which one of you is an economist?'

'I!' Che said and raised his hand.

'Good, then you'll be Governor! But you're a doctor, aren't you? When did you turn economist?'

'Oh, I thought you asked which one of us was a communist!'

Che Guevara checks industrial production.

Guevara laughed aloud, but neither confirmed nor denied the truth of the story.

At first he repeated several times that he liked cheerful people with a sense of humour and that he enjoyed funny stories, but he soon switched to a long and serious talk.

I.F. STONE: The word that first came to mind on meeting Che Guevara was simplicity. I had been waiting to see him for some time late at night in the Cuban National Bank building in Havana. He was the first man I had ever met whom I thought not just handsome, but beautiful. With his curly reddish beard, he looked like a cross between a faun and a Sunday-school print of Jesus. Mischief, zest, compassion and a sense of mission flashed across his features during our interview. But what struck me most of all was that he seemed in no way changed, corrupted or intoxicated by the power which had suddenly fallen into his hands. He spoke with that utter sobriety which sometimes masks immense apocalyptic visions. The focus of his political concern was not Moscow but his America – from the Mexican sierra to the Argentinian pampas – the America we forget when we enthnocentrically use the word in the United States. Of our

talk on that first visit, I remember the vivid relic of a fragile hope soon dissipated. 'We are going to be the Tito of the Caribbean,' Che said of the Castro regime. 'You get along with Tito and you will gradually reconcile yourself to getting along with us.' But accommodation with a rebel from the Russian empire was quite different from accommodation with a rebel from the American empire. American policy soon demonstrated that Castro would have to be Krushchev's *protégé*, if he were to survive our animosity. On my second visit, some weeks before the Bay of Pigs, there was no more talk of Titoism. Now Che spoke with enthusiasm of what he had seen in his grand tour of the Soviet bloc. What impressed him most was the reconstruction of North Korea and the quality of its industrial output – here was a tiny country resurrected from the ashes of American bombardment and invasion. Perhaps he saw this as a preview of Cuba's fate.

In February, 1961, the Ministry of Industry was established by the revolutionary government and Che Guevara was named Minister.

CHE: We cannot proclaim before the tomb of our martyrs that Cuba is independent economically. Cuba cannot be independent when just one

The hands of Che Guevara.

Che Guevara doing voluntary labour by machine during the sugar-cane harvest.

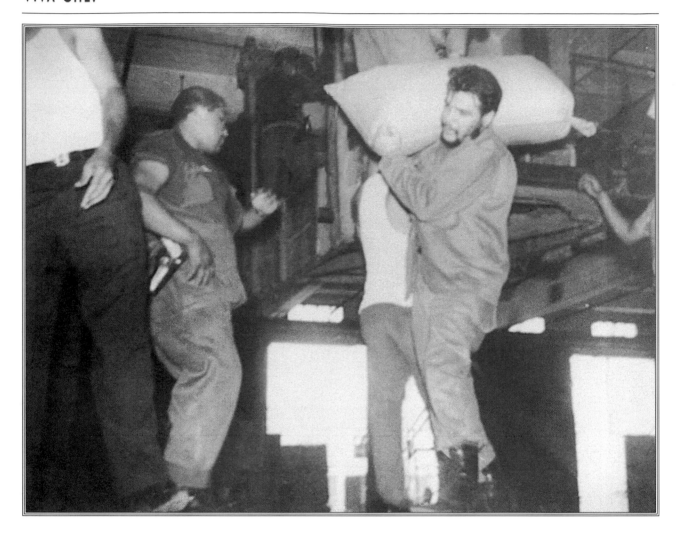

As Minister of the Interior, Che Guevara does voluntary labour.

Opposite: Che Guevara inspecting a mine, when he was Minister of Industry.

ship prevented from leaving the United States can make a factory go out of work in Cuba; when one simple order from any of the monopolies can paralyse a work centre here. Cuba will be independent when it has developed its natural wealth and when it has ensured by treaties and by commerce with all the world that no unilateral action by any foreign power can prevent it from maintaining its level of production and from keeping its factories going at full rate.

At this time, Fernando Barral wondered if the Cuban Major 'Che' Guevara could be his childhood friend, Ernesto. On enquiry, he received the followng reply from Che: 'Dear Fernando, I know you were not sure of my identity but suspected that it was not me. In fact, it was not, because a lot of water has flowed under my bridge and nothing remains of the asthmatic individual you once knew, apart from the asthma. I hear you are married. I am, too. I have two children, yet I remain an adventurer; only my adventures now have a truer purpose. This

survivor from the past sends your family greetings, and for you a friendly embrace from Che, which is henceforth my name.'

FERNANDO BARRAL: I saw him one evening at the Latino-Americano stadium where a Cuban team was playing against a Russian one. I went over to him and we sat together for the remainder of the match, after which we set off for the Ministry. We went by car. He was driving and as we passed through the crowd, people called out, 'Che, Che', catching him by the hand and trying to touch his clothes.

During the following years, Che dedicated himself as completely to the creation of a true economic and social revolution in Cuba as he had dedicated himself to the establishment of Castro's revolutionary régime. It was very hard work because, as he wrote, 'It is easy in moments of extreme peril to have recourse to moral incentives; but to maintain moral incentives at a high level at other times, new values have to be instilled into individual consciences. The whole of society has to be turned into a vast school. Underdevelopment on the one hand, and the withdrawal of capital to 'civilized' countries on the other hand, make impossible a rapid transformation without any sacrifices. We still have a great deal to do before we can reach a satisfactory level of economic development, and the temptation to have recourse to the old methods, to go back to the system of material incentives as a means of economic development, is very great. *But Che Guevara was also convinced that this had to be avoided at all costs because,* 'for man fully to realise himself, the concept of man as commodity must cease to exist, and society must give him his share in exchange for the accomplishment of a social duty. Man can attain his full stature only when he can produce without the physical necessity of selling himself like a piece of merchandise.' *Che always maintained that material obligations had to be turned into moral ones, or else men would continue to remain alienated from society and from their own natures.* 'We must create a new man who is neither left over from the 19th Century nor a product of our own corrupt and decadent century. It is the 21st Century man we must create.'

The attempt to reconcile the practical necessities of Cuba's economy with the theoretical aspirations implicit in the Revolution occupied all of Che's time. Every Sunday, he would leave for voluntary work in the fields or the factories. In 1964, he received a badge and a certificate for communist work for over 240 hours of voluntary production labour in a six-month period. He also wrote many articles, letters and books including 'Memoirs of the Revolutionary War', 'Guerrilla Warfare' and 'Man and Socialism in Cuba': in many speeches, he attempted to clarify the ideals that underlay his concepts.

CHE: 'If the revolutionary's ardour cools off once the most urgent tasks have been accomplished at the local scale, and if he forgets proletarian internationalism, the revolution itself ceases to be a force and settles back into a comfortable torpor which can be exploited by our irreconcilable enemies, the imperialists, who then gain ground.'

At some time during the Spring of 1965, Che Guevara disappeared from Cuba. Before he left he wrote several farewell letters.

TO FIDEL: Other nations in the world call for my modest efforts. I can do what you are prevented from doing by your responsibilities in Cuba, and the hour has come to part. . . .

. . . I say once again that I release Cuba from all responsibility except that of serving as my example. That if my final hour comes beneath other skies, my last thought will be for this people and especially for you. That I thank you for what you taught me and for your example, and that I will try to be true to my beliefs, whatever the final consequences. That I have always identified with the world outcome of our Revolution, and I am now following that path. That wherever I go, I will feel it is my duty to be a Cuban revolutionary, and to act as one. That I leave my wife and my children nothing, and I am not sorry, but glad it should be so. That I can do nothing for them as the State will give them enough to live on and will educate them.

I have many things to tell you and our people, but I feel they would be superfluous; words cannot express what I would wish to say. . . .

TO HIS PARENTS: Once more I feel Rosinante's flanks between my heels and so take to the road again, carrying my shield on my arm.

I believe that armed struggle is the only solution for those who are fighting to free themselves, and I am acting according to my convictions. Many will call me an adventurer, and I am one – only of a different sort, the sort who gamble their lives to prove what they believe. This time, the end may come. I do not seek it, but it is a logical possibility. Should this be so, this is my last embrace.

And now, a willpower which I have polished with an artist's love will sustain my weak legs and tired lungs. I will do it. Remember this minor twentieth-century *condottiere* from time to time and receive a kiss from your rebellious prodigal son.

TO ALBERTO GRANADOS: I don't know what to leave you as a remembrance. I force you, then, to spend a good long time in the sugar-cane. My roving house will have two legs once again, and my dreams will know no frontiers, at least until bullets speak. I expect you, sedentary gypsy, when the gunsmoke settles.

Che Guevara driving a tractor during the sugar-cane harvest, known as the Zafra.

Many rumours were in circulation after the departure of Che Guevara: it was said that he had been killed during the uprising in the Dominican Republic; that he was fighting in the Congo, in Vietnam, in Venezuela, in Laos. . . . No official news of him came until April, 1967, when a message was sent by him to the Tricontinental Solidarity Organisation in Havana.

CHE: . . . In Latin America, the armed struggle is going on in Guatamala, Colombia, Venezuela and Bolivia; the first uprisings are cropping up in Brazil. There are also some points of resistance which appear and then are extinguished. But almost all the countries in this continent are ready for a type of struggle that, in order to achieve victory, cannot be content with anything less than establishing a government of socialist tendencies. . . . New uprisings shall take place in these and other countries of our America, as it has already happened in Bolivia, and they shall continue to grow in the midst of all the hardships inherent to this dangerous profession of the modern revolutionary. Many shall perish, victims of their errors; others shall fall in the tough battle that is coming; new fighters and new leaders shall appear in the warmth of the revolutionary struggle. . . . We must take the war to every corner where the enemy happens to take it; to his home, to his places of entertainment; a total war. It is necessary to prevent him from having a moment of peace, a quiet moment outside his barracks or even inside; we must attack him wherever he may be; make him feel like a cornered beast wherever he may move. Then his moral fibre will begin to decline. He will become even more beastly, but we shall notice how the signs of decadence begin to appear. And let us develop a true proletarian internationalism, with international proletarian armies; the flag under which we fight would be the sacred cause of redeeming humanity. To die under the flag of Vietnam, of Venezuela, of Guatamala, of Laos, of Guinea, of Colombia, of Bolivia, of Brazil – to name only a few scenes of today's armed struggle – would be equally glorious and desirable for an American, an Asian, an African, even a European. Each drop of blood spilt by a man in any country under whose flag he was not born is an experience passed on to those who survive, to be added later to the liberation struggle of his own country. And each nation liberated is a phase won in the battle for the liberation of one's own country. The time has come to settle our disagreements and to put everything at the service of the struggle. . . . How close and brilliant the future would seem if two, three, many Vietnams flourished throughout the world with their share of deaths and their immense tragedies, their daily heroism and their repeated blows against imperialism, impelled to disperse its forces under the sudden attack and the increasing hatred of all peoples of the world!

. . . Wherever death may surprise us, let it be welcome, provided that this, our battle-cry, may have reached some receptive ear and

Opposite: Che Guevara with his machete, cutting the sugar-cane during the harvest.

another hand may be extended to wield our weapons and other men be ready to intone the funeral dirge with the staccato chant of the machine-gun and new battle-cries of war and victory.

Hasta la Victoria Siempre! Patria o Muerte, Venceremos!

On 8 October, 1967, in the region of Santa Cruz, Bolivia, a group of specially-trained Bolivian rangers was engaged in action against a unit of guerrillas, whom they had encircled. After a fierce battle, the rangers were able to capture the wounded guerrilla leader. He was taken to the nearby village of Higueras, where he was kept in a tiny school. After repeated attempts to interrogate him, he was shot through the heart towards noon of the following day. His corpse was strapped to the runners of a helicopter and taken to the nearby town of Vallegrande. There, it was exposed in a shack, where it was viewed by the local population, as well as journalists and photographers. It was announced to the world that this Bolivian guerrilla fighter, known as Ramón, was in fact Major Ernesto 'Che' Guevara. When Che's brother arrived in Bolivia to identify the body, he was told that the corpse had been incinerated and the ashes scattered.

MARIANNE ALEXANDRE

Song for Fidel
by Che Guevara

Let's go,
Fiery prophet of the dawn,
Down winding secret paths,
To free the green land that you love.

Let's go,
To avenge many wrongs,
Our foreheads full of rebel stars,
Swearing to win or die.

When the first shot is heard and the land wakes up,
Like a girl startled out of sleep,
We'll be there by your side, calm warriors,
We'll be there.

When your voice proclaims to the four winds
Land reform, justice, bread and freedom,
We'll be there to echo your words,
We'll be there.

The day the wild beast is wounded in its side
By our liberating aim,
We'll be with you, hearts full of pride,
We'll be there.

Don't think that they can make us tremble,
Armed with gifts and decorations,
We want a rifle, bullets, a stick,
Nothing more.

And if their rifles mow us down,
We only ask for Cuban tears
As winding sheets for fighters
Washed away by the flow of history,
Nothing more.

Contributions in Tribute to Ernesto 'Che' Guevara

The *baas* thinks
When it comes
Napalm tanks
Wire dum-dums
Shrapnel whips
Electric shocks
Booby traps
Will block us

The *baas* thinks
Flesh and blood
Sinew flanks
Black and red
Shall not stand
The war machine
The steel wind
The iron whine

Che, now our fingers are propellors
Cities burn where our minds were numb
Our arms are the barrels of mortars
Our heads are fused like a bomb

You have turned our tribes to brigades
We flow remorseless where rivers ran
Our loins are the seed of grenades
Our ribs are the armoury of man

After you, we will never yield
We have one thing to give you, a life
And the bullet shall break on our shield
And the vulture shall fall on our knife

The *baas* fears
When it comes
We'll wash our spears
In blood and bones
But Che knows
It comes soon . . .
The white night grows . . .
See the black moon!

J.A. (South Africa)

What I felt, as a human being, on hearing of Che's death, was influenced by the experience of some years in socialist countries of Eastern Europe. In the People's Poland, for instance, where flats may be got in reasonable time only by paying in dollars, where I have heard of prosperous Party members being bribed for a place in a sanatorium, and where everything stagnates, there is a good deal of noble talk, on all the media, about revolutionary heroes, and this – if nothing else – has killed my romanticism.

I have never been to Latin America, but I have read, in books by moderate writers, of a feudalism ranging from an outdated paternalism to a reign of terror. I have heard of wooden ploughs dodging round boulders on semi-barren hillsides and hunger allayed by manioc and bad coffee. In London I have mixed with irresponsible sons of the big landowners.

The revolution I really believe in is non-violent, but obviously to dictate non-violence to classes or races in a desperate plight is outrageously silly. I admire not only Che's courage and skill but his insistence that without a firm moral basis there can be no real revolution. Che's revolution won't triumph easily; his enemies have also studied his book and developed devastating tactics of counter-insurgency. But it will triumph in the end, and I hope for the emergence in Latin America of free, healthy, vivid societies without that canker of so many 'socialist' countries, a selfish élite of old ex-partisans and young technologists.

JOHN ADLARD (England)

To the Memory of Che

beneath the white map
or chaos
of the stars
the moon floats

he stands barefoot
on the cracked
warm earth
nightbirds shriek

swoop
his mineral sweat
makes luminous
his fear

he waits to kill
a tank
with an old gun
that his father

killed rabbits with
and a broken-
bladed knife
but no tank appears

so at dawn he turns
to go and two
soldiers
shoot him twice

walk away
not talking
buttoning
their pistol holsters

and when the sun
makes salt
from his sweat
and he lies dying

in the flat field
nursing his
torn belly
he tries to say

LYMAN ANDREWS (USA)

Here we are
appalled
outraged
even though this death is
one of the foreseeable absurdities

I'm ashamed to look at
the paintings
the armchairs
the carpets
to take a bottle out of the refrigerator
to tap out the three universal letters of your name
in the rigid machine
that never
never had
so pale a ribbon

Shame to feel the cold
and get near the stove as usual
to be hungry and eat
such a simple thing
to turn on the gramophone and listen in silence
to a Mozart quartet most of all

Shame on the comfort
shame on the asthma
when you comandante are falling
riddled
fabulous
brilliant
our conscience is full of holes

I hear that they burnt you
with what fire
are they going to burn the good
the glad tidings
the inexorable tenderness
that you brought with you and left behind
with your cough
and your earthenware cup
I hear that they burnt
all your vocation
minus a finger

enough to point out the way to us
and to accuse the monster who defiled you
and to tighten other fingers on the trigger

and so here we are
appalled
outraged

Sure that in time the leaden
amazement
will wear off
but the rage will remain
and its contours grow sharper

you are dead
you are living
you are falling
you are a cloud
you are the rain
you are a star

Where are you
if you are
if you are arriving
take off a moment at last
to breathe peacefully
to fill your lungs with sky

where are you
if you are
if you are arriving
it will be a pity if God does not exist

but there will be others
there are sure to be others
fit to welcome you
comandante.

MARIO BENEDETTI (Uruguay)

On Tuesday 10 October, 1967, a photograph was transmitted to the world to prove that Guevara had been killed the previous Sunday in a clash between two companies of the Bolivian army and a guerrilla force on the north side of the Rio Grande river near a jungle village called Higueras. (Later this village received the proclaimed reward for the capture of Guevara.) The photograph of the corpse was taken in a stable in the small town of Vallegrande. The body was placed on a stretcher and the stretcher was placed on top of a cement trough.

During the preceding two years 'Che' Guevara had become legendary. Nobody knew for certain where he was. There was no incontestable evidence of anyone having seen him. But his presence was constantly assumed and invoked. At the head of his last statement – sent from a guerrilla base 'somewhere in the world' to the Tri-continental Solidarity Organisation in Havana – he quoted a line from the 19th century revolutionary Cuban poet José Martí: 'Now is the time of the furnaces, and only light should be seen.' It was as though in his own declared light Guevara had become invisible and ubiquitous.

Now he is dead. The chances of his survival were in inverse ratio to the force of the legend. The legend had to be nailed. 'If,' said the *New York Times*, 'Ernesto Che Guevara was really killed in Bolivia, as now seems probable, a myth as well as a man has been laid to rest.'

We do not know the circumstances of his death. One can gain some idea of the mentality of those into whose hands he fell by their treatment of his body after his death. First they hid it. Then they displayed it. Then they buried it in an anonymous grave in an unknown place. Then they disinterred it. Then they burnt it. But before burning it, they cut off the fingers for later identification. This might suggest that they had serious doubts whether it was really Guevara whom they had killed. Equally it can suggest that they had no doubts, but feared his corpse. I tend to believe the latter.

The purpose of the radio photograph of 10 October was to put an end to a legend. Yet on many who saw it, its effect may have been very different. What is its meaning? What, precisely and unmysteriously, does the photograph mean now? I can but cautiously analyse it as regards myself.

There is a resemblance between the photograph and Rembrandt's painting of *The Anatomy Lesson of Professor Tulp*. The immaculately dressed Bolivian colonel has taken the professor's place. The two figures on his left stare at the cadaver with the same intense but impersonal interest as the two nearest doctors on the professor's left. It is true that there are more figures in the Rembrandt – as there were certainly more men, unphotographed, in the stable at Vallegrande. But the placing of the corpse in relation to the figures above it, and in the corpse the sense of global stillness – these are very similar.

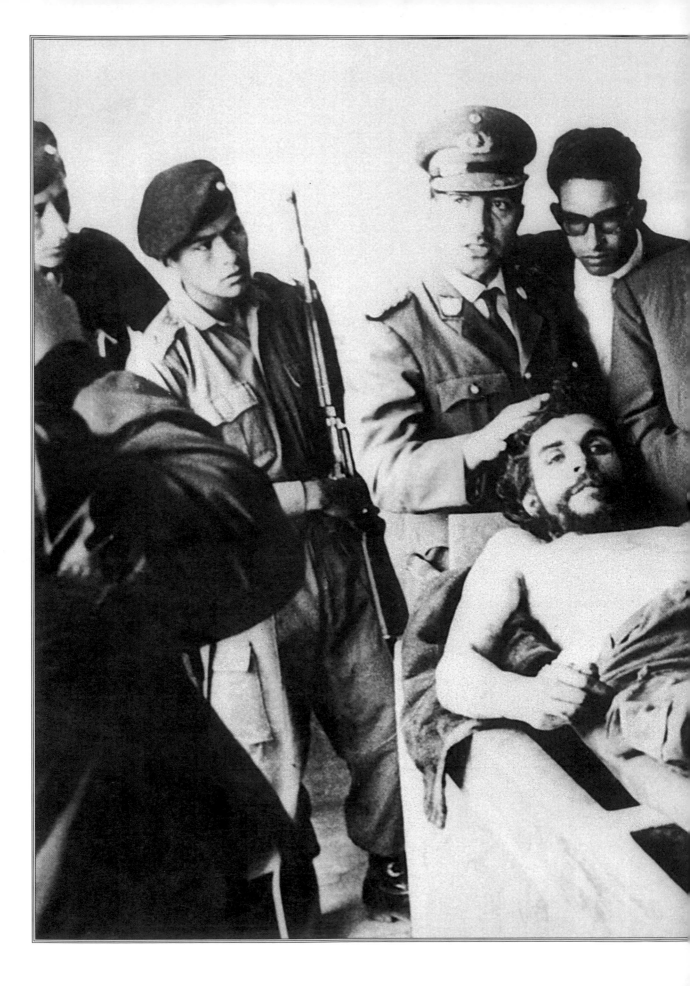

Bolivian officers, soldiers and journalists in the town of Vallegrande, inspecting the dead body of Che Guevara.

Nor should this be surprising, for the function of the two pictures is similar: both are concerned with showing a corpse being formally and objectively examined. More than that, both are concerned with *making an example of the dead*: one for the advancement of medicine, the other as a political warning. Thousands of photographs are taken of the dead and the massacred. But the occasions are seldom formal ones of demonstration. Doctor Tulp is demonstrating the ligaments of the arm, and what he says applies to the normal arm of every man. The colonel is demonstrating the final fate – as decreed by 'divine providence'- of a notorious guerrilla leader, and what he says is meant to apply to every guerrilla on the continent.

I was also reminded of another image: Mantegna's painting of the dead Christ, now in the Brera at Milan. The body is seen from the same height, but from the feet instead of from the side. The hands are in identical positions, the fingers curving in the same gesture. The drapery over the lower part of the body is creased and formed in the same manner as the blood-sodden, unbuttoned, olive-green trousers on Guevara. The head is raised at the same angle. The mouth is slack of expression in the same way. Christ's eyes have been shut, for there are two mourners beside him. Guevara's eyes are open, for there are no mourners: only the colonel, a US intelligence agent, a number of Bolivian soldiers and the thirty journalists. Once again, the similarity need not surprise. There are not so many ways of laying out the criminal dead.

Yet this time the similarity was more than gestural or functional. The emotions with which I came upon that photograph on the front page of the evening paper on that Wednesday afternoon were very close to what, with the help of historical imagination, I had previously assumed the reaction of a contemporary believer might have been to Mantegna's painting. The power of a photograph is comparatively short-lived. When I look at the photograph now, I can only reconstruct my first incoherent emotions. Guevara was no Christ. If I see the Mantegna again in Milan, I shall see in it the body of Guevara. But this is only because in certain rare cases the tragedy of a man's death completes and exemplifies the meaning of his whole life. I am acutely aware of that about Guevara, and certain painters were once aware of it about Christ. That is the degree of emotional correspondence.

The mistake of many commentators on Guevara's death has been to suppose that he represented only his military skill or a certain revolutionary strategy. Thus they talk of a setback or a defeat. I am in no position to assess the loss which Guevara's death may mean to the revolutionary movement in South America. But it is certain that Guevara represented and will represent more than the details of his plans. He represented a decision, a conclusion.

Guevara found the condition of the world as it is intolerable. It had only recently become so. Previously, the conditions under which two-thirds of the people of the world lived were approximately the same as now. The degree of exploitation and enslavement was as great. The suffering involved was as intense and as widespread. The waste was as colossal. But it was not intolerable because the full measure of the truth about the condition was unknown – even by those who suffered it. Truths are not constantly evident in the circumstances to which they refer. They are born – sometimes late. This truth was born with the struggles and wars of national liberation. In the light of the newborn truth, the significance of imperialism changed. Its demands were seen to be different. Previously it had demanded cheap raw materials, exploited labour and a controlled world market. Today it demands a mankind that counts for nothing.

Guevara envisaged his own death in the revolutionary fight against this imperialism. 'Wherever death may surprise us, let it be welcome, provided that this, our battle-cry, may have reached some receptive ear and another hand may be extended to wield our weapons and other men be ready to intone the funeral dirge with the staccato chant of the machine-gun and new battle-cries of war and victory.'

His envisaged death offered him the measure of how intolerable his life would be if he accepted the intolerable condition of the world as it is. His envisaged death offered him the measure of the necessity of changing the world. It was by the licence granted by his envisaged death that he was able to live with the necessary pride that becomes a man.

At the news of Guevara's death, I heard someone say: 'He was the world symbol of the possibilities of one man.' Why is this true? Because he recognised what was tolerable for man and acted accordingly.

The measure by which Guevara had lived, suddenly became a unit which filled the world and obliterated his life. His envisaged death became actual. The photograph is about this actuality. The possibilities have gone. Instead there is blood, the smell of formol, the untended wound on the unwashed body, flies, the shambling trousers: the small private details of the body rendered in dying as public and impersonal and broken as a razed city.

Guevara died surrounded by his enemies. What they did to him while he was alive was probably consistent with what they did to him after he was dead. In his extremity he had nothing to support him but his own previous decisions. Thus the cycle was closed. It would be the vulgarest impertinence to claim any knowledge of his experience during that instant or that eternity. His lifeless body, as seen in the photograph, is the only report we have. But we are entitled to deduce the logic of what happens when the cycle closes. Truth flows in the obverse direction. His envisaged death is no more the measure of the necessity for changing the intolerable condition of the world. Aware now of his actual death, he finds in his life the measure of his justification, and the world-as-his-experience becomes tolerable to him.

The foreseeing of this final logic is part of what enables a man or a people to fight against overwhelming odds. It is part of the secret of the moral factor which counts as three to one against weapon power.

The photograph shows an instant: that instant at which Guevara's body, artificially preserved, has become a mere object of demonstration. In this lies its initial horror. But what is it intended to demonstrate? Such horror? No. It is to demonstrate, at the instant of horror, the identity of Guevara and, allegedly, the absurdity of revolution. Yet by virtue of this very purpose, the instant is transcended. The life of Guevara and the idea or fact of revolution immediately invoke processes which preceded that instant and which continue now. Hypothetically, the only way in which the purpose of those who arranged for and authorised the photograph could have been achieved, would have been to preserve artificially at that instant the whole state of the world as it was: to stop life. Only in such a way could the content of Guevara's living example have been denied. As it is, either the photograph means nothing because the spectator has no inkling of what is involved, or else its meaning denies or qualifies its demonstration.

I have compared it with two paintings, because paintings, before the invention of photography, are the only visual evidence we have of how people saw what they saw. But in its effect it is profoundly different from a painting. A painting, or a successful one at least, comes to terms with the processes invoked by its subject matter. It even suggests an attitude towards those processes. We can regard a painting as almost complete in itself.

In face of this photograph we must either dismiss it, or complete its meaning for ourselves. It is an image which, as much as any mute image ever can, calls for decision.

JOHN BERGER (England)

Speaking of Che

Now Che no longer lives, it's true,
Che has died, comrade repeat
but also repeat what I say with you:
that the enemy is trembling.

Let's sing, not for a fiesta,
but to prepare for the hard struggle ahead
every death must be paid for, comrades,
the enemy has to pay the price

Hard has been the luck
of this rich downtrodden continent
until the day the rifle flame
sets the land alight
and claims its just reward

That rifle won't fall silent for a minute
for if the firm hand
of Che has let go
another hand is sure to take it up.
Only the bullet matters
and the thought that directs its course.

We have bullets, we have rifles,
we have determined guerrillas,
they know where they are marching,
even in sorrow their hearts rejoice;
the enemy's luck will run out,
and his fate is to die in darkness

People will call out the names
of the enemies, of the ruthless officers,
of the Yankees with their war machines,
of the bosses who own the money and the wheels,
the plantations and the land.

And we, who are we?
We are all the poor and the beaten,
the humiliated but determined
poor but worthiest inhabitants
of this volcanic continent.

With Che we go through ragged valleys
through prairies and through cities.
We will carry on until
One day we set fire to the mountain

We're not complaining nor asking for anything
from our oppressors
we will never argue with them.
We will travel, comandante, along the bullet's path
and wander from one battle to the next.

And what are we fighting for,
and why so ready to make the sacrifice,
if not for the love of bread and fruits,
for the sweat of the common people,
for a dawn of American love
for a day of victory and socialism?

Che said in his guerrilla's language
death is a concept
which comes up a thousand times over
and victory is the myth
of the guerrilla's dreams;
in his deep hard sleep
he reckons on his dream

Tell me, comandante,
where are all the leaders
to go on with the fight?
and where are the future warriors?
Some are already struggling
others are being born among the leaves and by the rivers,
they are being nourished by their earth and their sky,
which are yours too, comandante, as well as mine.

Quickly, back into battle,
the fight must not ease up,
our weapons glitter redly,
as we go forward, burning with sacred hatred.

We will be worthy, comandante,
we swear it by the revolution!

SARANDY CABRERA (Uruguay)

Whatever I might try to write to express my admiration for Ernesto Che Guevara, living or dead, seems unreal to me. I hear his laughter, full of irony and commiseration answering me. I am here, sitting in my study, surrounded by my books, in the false peace and the false prosperity of Europe, and I devote a brief interval in my daily labours, to write without risk, about a man who wanted to take on himself all the risks, who had not accepted the pretence of a temporary peace, a man who demanded of himself, as of others, the greatest spirit of sacrifice, convinced that every hesitation to sacrifice today would cost far greater sacrifice tomorrow. For us, Guevara is this call to the ultimate seriousness of everything concerning the revolution and the future of the world, this radical criticism of every gesture which serves to appease our conscience.

In this sense he remains the centre of our discussions and our thoughts, no less in death than in life. He is a presence which does not demand from us facile approval nor formal acts of homage: this would result in misunderstanding and minimising the extreme rigour of his lesson. The 'code of Che' demands much from men, no less in

Che Guevara in his office at the Ministry.

the manner of the struggle than in the perspective of the society which should be born out of the struggle. As against the courage and coherence needed to take a thought and a way of life to its ultimate conclusion, let us show ourselves first of all modest and sincere, aware of what the 'code of Che' means – a total transformation not only of society but of human nature, starting from ourselves – and aware of what separates us from putting it into practice.

Guevara's discussion with all those surrounding him, the long discussion which was his short life – from discussion to action to discussion without ever abandoning the gun – will not be interrupted by death. It will always continue to grow. So for an occasional and unknown questioner as I was, with a group of guests one afternoon in 1964 in his office in the Ministry of Industry, meeting him could not remain a marginal episode. The discussions that matter are those that go on silently in the mind. In my mind, the discussions with Che have gone on all these years, and the more time has passed, the more he has been right. And now, having died setting in motion a struggle which cannot stop, he will ever continue to be more and more right.

ITALO CALVINO (Italy)

Two names, above all others, sum up the new age of South America: Ernesto 'Che' Guevara and Camilo Torres Restrepo.*

Both were heroes and both were martyrs. Both dedicated themselves to the same cause: the liberation of their people. And when I speak of their 'people,' I mean the oppressed, the exploited, the poor and the hungry.

The same flame burned in their hearts and gave them a heroic calling. They knew very well that they could put their youth to the service of freedom and that is what they had to do.

They believed that a political system which does not help the masses must be overthrown, and that a more equitable government, better adapted to resolve the problem of poverty, must be established in its place.

In temporal terms, the Christian ideal is to serve the poor and the down-trodden. It is an inhuman and wretched thing to drag out a life devoid of hope, due to the fault of a social order which cannot resolve the basic needs of man. The people of Latin America are being crushed by the ruling oligarchies and imperialism. El Che and Father Camilo rebelled against imperialistic domination because it represents a threat both to individuals and to underdeveloped nations.

* *The revolutionary Colombian priest who was killed in action, fighting with the Columbian guerrillas on 15 February, 1966.*

To die so that men will recover hope and start struggling to win real freedom is a Christian act. Both Che Guevara and Father Camilo gave their lives for a Christian ideal. Both stand for the ultimate expression of Justice, which is one of the fundamental tenets of Christianity.

I agree with Olivier Maillard when he claims that the fight for justice, the sacrifice of one's life for one's brothers, the generosity of an undertaking, are all evangelical realities, all genuine attempts to bring about the true reign of God on earth. Camilo and Che were helping to bring about this reign by their fight for equal justice for all. They understood that this was their mission, preached, fought and died for it without a trace of opportunism.

They never made any compromise or tried to barter with their consciences. They merely accepted all the consequences which their beliefs entailed, as those beliefs were derived from logical convictions too self-evident to be debated.

Both were highly educated and had a powerful personality. Both were born leaders. Their most outstanding characteristic was their unconditional renunciation of everything, in order to serve the best of causes. Their home was all South America, that vast continent which cries out for justice.

They became revolutionaries and guerrilla fighters because imperialism leads to violence, feeds on violence, is born of violence, and can only be fought with violence. Like all other revolutionaries, Che Guevara and Father Camilo were the offspring of the time and circumstance of their continent.

Che Guevara and Father Camilo are both symbols and prophets of our age. They redeem it with their blood and their example. They died to redeem the times we live in. They set off for the mountains and stayed there, new Christs of the new Christianity. The soldiers hid their bodies in an unknown place, for tyrants fear the bones of heroes. Heroes, even dead, burn only too brightly, while tyrants carry their curse everywhere branded on their foreheads.

Heroes like Che Guevara and Camilo Torres are born when they die; tyrants die when they are born, for they are nothing more than walking corpses. They and their so-called democracies are a negation of every value, while men like Che and Camilo are completely authentic. Their voice, their wounds, their inner fire continue to urge the wretched of the earth to fight, because it is necessary to fight.

When the history of the revolution is written, it will be divided into two parts: the period which preceded the deaths of Che and Camilo, and the period which came after their ultimate sacrifice. From now on, the history of America is split into two halves.

GERMAN GUZMAN CAMPOS (Colombia)

Che Guevara,
many people asked you?
Where is your real home?
And you replied:
My home is where I can fight the revolution.

Your home is where people suffer,
and you can join in their struggle.
Oh, Che, your home is America,
and the footprints you leave on your way to battle
trace the frontiers of your country.
For guerrillas on the march, all day all night,
outline the map of their true nationality.

There, wherever humanity cries out
and its anger catches fire,
and it strikes out at the enemy,
there is your home.
It's true, Che, that you were born
in one specific point in space;
but your heart made you a citizen
of all the horizons of life.

And Cuba, what about Cuba?
Cuba is the home of my heart.
Yet for the sake of the revolution
I gave up my duties, my home and my house.
I even gave up my nationality,
to set off again, taking only the uniform
I had worn in bygone days.
But Cuba will always be mingled
with all of me, each drop of blood;
so how can I really part from Cuba?
Oh, Fidel, Cuba is home!

And Vietnam, what about Vietnam?
Vietnam is a land I never went to,
and yet I have been there. With its selflessness and its sacrifice,
my heart is there in the line of fire.
And what the world needs is at least two or three
or more Vietnams. You once said this,
and meant it . . .
As you blew on the coals of the revolution,
until they grew red and glowed.

And now, Che Guevara,
you have fallen on that path of fire and blood;
while you were forging real homes for people,
you were struck down on the road you had chosen.
And as you fell your long arms stretched out to the whole of America.
There are millions left to love you,
and hearts everywhere to remember you,
all those who love the people and the truth you loved.
Some names fill us with pride in humanity.
Some fighters can go on giving strength when they have fallen;
which is why you, Oh, Che, are with us right now in the battle-line.

CU HUY CAN (North Vietnam)

The death of Che Guevara places a responsibility on all revolutionaries of the world to redouble their decision to fight on to the final defeat of imperialism. This is not the time to make long speeches dedicated to Che's memory, but a time for practical, courageous action. . . .

Che explained clearly that there is no need to talk more, that the contradictions in the world are clear, and that the time has come for each to take his place in the fight. . . .

That is why – in essence – Che Guevara is not dead. I do not wish to speak of Che as if he were dead. It would not make sense. His ideas are with us.

I never met Che Guevara in person, but I know him. And I know him even better now. The important thing is to realise that his ideas are with us, and that is why we are prepared to go on fighting.

STOKELY CARMICHAEL (USA)

Che's life has had the virtue of impressing even his worst ideological enemies and making them admire him. It is an almost unique example of how a man has been able to gain the recognition and respect of his enemies, of the very troops whom he has faced arms in hand; of his ideological enemies, who have been, surprisingly, almost unanimous in expressing feelings of admiration for Che.

Who could deny the significance to the revolutionary movement of the blow of Che's death, the significance of not being able to count upon his experience, his inspiration, upon that strength of his prestige that all reactionaries feared? It is a fierce blow, a very hard one; however, we are sure that he, more than anyone, was convinced that it is not the physical life of men, but their conduct which counts. That alone can explain his own absolute scorn for danger. That alone accounts for his personality and his actions. . . .

Che was unsurpassed both as a leader and as a soldier; militarily speaking, he was an extraordinarily able, courageous and warlike guerrilla. His one weak spot was that he was too brave and too indifferent to danger.

His enemies now claim to see a moral in the fact that he should have died. But Che was an artist in guerrilla warfare; he proved it a thousand times over. And yet there are now some to suggest that his glorious and heroic death proves that his concepts and his theories on guerrilla warfare were neither valid nor correct.

The artist can die, especially when his art is the dangerous art of revolutionary warfare, but what cannot possibly die is the art to which he dedicated his life and his intelligence.

Is it surprising that such an artist as Che should die in battle? What is far more astonishing is that he should have survived so many battles during our revolutionary war in which he risked his life countless times. . . .

Che did not die defending any interest or cause other than that of the exploited and downtrodden of this continent. Che died defending that cause alone, and even his worst enemies have not dared to suggest otherwise.

Seen in historical terms, those who act as Che did, who do all they can and who sacrifice everything to the cause of the needy, cannot fail to grow in significance every day and to sink deeper and deeper into the hearts of the people.

FIDEL CASTRO (Cuba)

There will be poems in his memory. But the grinding predicament of *les damnés de la terre* is not lyrical. Nor even the struggle against it, which was Guevara's struggle. Guerrilla warfare, as he explained, is slow, patient, prosaic. It is technical.

Revolutions too are technical. They run the same risks as speculative machines. History defines their rules and their possibilities. It is common knowledge – Castro knew it, Che knew it – that in the past the moment of victory has often masked the moment of defeat. Batista (the king, the tsar, the Kuomintang) are negligible enemies compared to bonapartism and bureaucracy, the hookworms which linger for years in the entrails of the triumphant revolution.

In Cuba the Fidelistas – the authentic originals whose idealism was imperishable and whose ideology was relatively eclectic – have remained indispensable to the integrity of the revolution. They have stood between the people and the opportunists and placemen, the new class: who also suffered in their time.

Yet while Castro stayed, Che departed. Of course, he was not a Cuban. And he could not rest while the United States loomed over Latin America like an umbrella, dripping with greed. Asian communism had made the century its own; the millions had surfaced. So Che abandoned the revolution in favour of the revolution.

Garibaldi, in his greatness, was comic and flamboyant. His insurgents wore red shirts and sang while they marched. Che moved patiently and reflectively, like an underground river. Byronic, certainly. But he also embodied the technique of the age. In Che temperament and social strategy converged. In order to win, he vanished, fell silent, except to the people he went among, who are known to us only as statistics and as possible inhabitants of a landscape which can be seen from an aeroplane.

Not by any stretch of paradox can his failure be called a success. The dialectic is not a conjuror. One cannot even say: his memory and example will live on, like Garibaldi's. That is not enough, for Garibaldi's cause was never won.

DAVID CAUTE (England)

Ballad

Where the dry river runs
The soldiers took their time;
He could not breathe or climb
When they ringed him in their guns

Two soldiers scrubbed
The school where he was shot
For farmers who could not
Read might read in blood:

And those who live by the word will die by the sword
And their bodies will be burned either alive or dead
Like a new book that must not be read
By a people who should never have been taught to read
Because the word of law and order is the only book they need

Mother mother see your son
What do his wounds say
Only he should not have gone
Not have gone to play

Out beyond the streets we know
Out beyond the town
Till the bullets that he sowed
Grew up in a thousand guns to cut him down

He could have lived by the word and shunned the sword
And his body would have been cherished alive or dead
He could have written books that would have been read and read
By later children who'd have learned to read
Because time to grow is all a child and all a world need

But where could he find rest?
Writing in the east
Hunted by the police
Tortured till he confessed

Where those who live by the word are tried by the sword
And their bodies are buried either alive or dead
Like a new book that must not be read
By a people who oughtn't to be free to read
Because the word of law and order is the only book they need

Or here in the easy west,
Where he could live at least
Writing books in peace
Well fed and well dressed

Where those who live by the word are afraid of the word
And their bodies are constricted alive or dead
By a dread they won't be read or won't be fit to be read

Out beyond the streets we know
Out beyond the town
Till the bullets that he sowed
Grew up in a thousand guns to cut him down

And yet the dead man still
Is with his wounds alive
Will with his wounds survive
The dictator's will
And the rich man's mind
Who when he will not give
To let the poor man live
Turns and sees behind
A man with a broken knife

A man not pure or good
A slaughtered man, whose blood
Pays for the rich man's life
Pays for the rich man's life

ALASDAIR CLAYRE (England)

Fleet through the forest trees
Ran Che Guevara
Moccasined were his feet
Round his cigar a
Beard curled in devil's horns
Brushed by the clutching thorns
Soundless he rushed, a breeze
Shaking the mighty seat
Of McNamara

Camped in the Mountain's heart
With his guerrillas
Bold Che Guevara sat
In his stone pillars
Taunting the Government
Mocking the Conscripts sent
To tear his world apart
Somewhere a rifle spat
Che faced his killers

Men from the C.I.A.
Knives in their garter
Fell on the hero band
Dreaming of Sparta
Loosed off a fusillade
Swift through the Everglade
In brown Bolivian clay
Cuba's bright star, outmanned,
Died like a martyr

DON COLLIS (England)

*Companion of my soul, I want to be the
weeping gardener of the soil that covers
you and that, so young, you feed.*

MIGUEL HERNÁNDEZ

So that your corpse may not be the end of you
or your bones a pile of stubble, useful to the tree
that must grow where you rot, sleeping soundly,
your universal heart pumping blood in and out
so as not to cry like defenceless orphans in corners
so as not just to sit here, in our minds avenging your loss
on this night, this irremediable night that almost chokes us,
so that you should not have missed the point nor made a bet
in which you lost the lucky number of the victory,
we shall now print your name upon this date.

I want to say that you exist in a way
which is the opposite of existence as we know it,
neither austere nor aggressive, merely silent.
There is no life there, no shouting and fighting,
no manifestos to organize;
they don't have beards there, nor legendary heroes.
It is a life we recreate for you so that we need not face
the sight of you, broken and stiff and dead.
This is the only tolerable theory,
everything else hurts too much;
as if they had cut off a limb from each of us.
Our feet go nowhere, only towards the memory
you left behind, the popular cemetery where you are buried
a second time, with your wide-open eyes.
The head is useless, we can't bear it on our shoulders,
it rolled with you when your luck ran out.

They defeated you once guerrilla,
but only once, not more
just enough time to arm our suffering
with tears and everything you need to kill.
Your death starts another cycle of anger,
we are going to recover your heritage bullet by bullet,
each footprint marked by your boot on the American woodland,
your asthma with open mouth, your love that sustains us,
your violence and your indispensable hatred,
your throat full of tender words.

I Salute you man of God!
though you will not listen to the arrogance
of a man who loves every bit of you.
We will never see you again
dreaming of continents.

Sustain our vengeance from that solitude,
from that mineral deep where the mystery is denser.
One fruitful, luminous day . . .
YOUR GREAT ADVENTURE WILL SWEEP THE WORLD.
There immortality resides,
companion of my soul, companion,
hasta la victoria siempre.

ANTONIO CONTE (Cuba)

Now words will be written, useless words, eloquent words, dictated by tears or by anger; now beautiful images will be composed about phoenixes rising from the ashes; now there will be poems and discussions which will be dedicated to the image of Che. I'm writing words too, but I don't want my words to be like those. I don't want to be someone writing words about him. I ask for the impossible, that which I least deserve, that which I dared do once when he was alive: I ask that it be his voice recorded here, that it be his hand that writes these lines. I know this is absurd, impossible; and that is exactly why I feel he is writing these lines with me, because no one knew better than he to what extent the absurd, the impossible, would one day become a reality for mankind, that future for which he gave his young, his marvellous life. Use my hand once more, then, my brother. It has done them no good to cut off your hands, it has done them no good to kill you and hide you away with such infamous cunning. Take my pen, and write. What I say and do I will say and do with you at my side. Only thus does it make sense to go on living.

JULIO CORTAZAR (Argentina)

I want to point out, first of all, that Guevara's death does not mean the end of the struggle against imperialism so much as its beginning; for his death has inexorably furnished a flag to fight under.

Because Che is not one of those who can die – as an example and a guide, he is immortal – because he will live on in the heart of each revolutionary.

One Che has died: others are about to be born or on the point of acting: others are already in action or will enter the stage tomorrow, here and in other parts of the continent. . . .

A civilian lawyer expressed the fear that the defence would ask for clemency, thus depriving the victors of their right to judge the vanquished. But who is asking for clemency? Who presumes to talk in terms of victors? Who admits to being vanquished? Che vanquished because he died? For years, Che had been exposing his life and escaping death by a miracle; years ago, he decided to fight in the front line wherever he might be needed, here and elsewhere; years ago, Che accepted the prospect of dying at any moment. He used to say that his sacrifice would mean nothing, that it would be no more than one incident in the course of world revolution, and that it was up to every one of us to turn his blood into seed. Some men are more dangerous dead than alive, even when those who fear them cut the hands from their corpse, burn the body and hide the ashes. Che comes to life for us now, and the revolution goes on.

No, I will not ask for the clemency of the vanquished. I will not address myself to you as to the victors. On the contrary, I will say to you that, even though I feel I am completely innocent of all the charges you have brought against me, I am guilty of believing in the final and imminent victory of Che. I am guilty of wanting to fulfil the engagement which I contracted towards him, irrevocably; as everyone who had the privilege of seeing Che live, think and act, felt engaged within his limitations to remain loyal to Che and to follow his example, until the end.

I will do all I can to deserve some day the unwarranted honour which you do me when you condemn me for doing what I did not do but which I want, more than ever, to do. And so, calmly and with all my heart, I thank you in advance for the heavy sentence that I expect from you.

I have finished.

REGIS DEBRAY (France), *at his trial at Camiri in November, 1967.*

Che was the first man to show us that we could be disgusted with peaceful co-existence without falling into the trap of right-wing opportunism, that we could reject the petty-bourgeois Marxism of local elections and 'deals' and still remain communists. Above all, he was the first to proclaim loudly and clearly that socialism is worth nothing when it is limited to an economic doctrine which only makes a more rational use of 'the worn-out tools of capitalism,' but what we have to fight for is a socialism which will create a new humanity. We also have Che to thank for the fact that the Cuban Revolution, which gave us new faith and courage in 1959, has continued to remain so dear to our hearts.

Che stands for romanticism without illusions; he stands for the greatest love, that which cannot limit itself to one woman, one man, one family. He is the mad and reasonable love which leads a man to fight on foreign soil, which leads a Jew to fight for the Arabs, a Frenchman to fight for the Algerians, a white man to fight for the negroes, and a bourgeois to fight for the proletariat. . . .

I can still hear the first thing he ever said to me, nearly seven years

Che Guevara examines military preparedness.

ago when I met him in Cuba, at the Bay of Pigs during the invasion. 'What are you doing here, Francesa?' I gave him a vague explanation . . . 'Paris boring, nothing happening politically. . . .' In that friendly and ironic way of his, he answered, 'But if you can't do anything in France, why not go and fight for the Algerians, who haven't got their independence yet?' Three years later in Algiers, after Algerian independence, he reminded me of this. 'What are you doing here now? They're free. They don't need you any more.' He also said to me once, 'You like success, what has been won already. You only write about what's victorious. You should fight for a cause which is only just starting, which seems likely to fail. . . .'

It was difficult not to feel shy with him even when you knew him well; you did not feel like using the familiar 'tu' with him, even though everyone addresses the Cuban leaders like that. There was something extraordinarily calm and gentle about Che; his voice was very low, slightly hoarse. I think he was a bit shy himself. What was odd was the contrast between his athletic, muscular frame, and his excessively delicate, aristocratic features, his pale, almost sickly complexion. He was as handsome and attractive as people have made him out to be, but it was not so much his good looks as his expression, so intelligent, kind and humorous, which gave him such charm. He always wore an olive green uniform, thick laced-up boots and a black beret pulled right down over his eyes, never wearing anything else throughout his stay in Paris in 1964. Yet he always looked very neat and never seemed to be in 'fancy dress.' I remember the contrast between his way of dressing and Ben Bella's when we were in Algiers, at the height of China's prestige. Ben Bella wore a uniform which was a curious cross between Nehru's and Mao's, and which Che glanced at with amusement and surprise.

When Che looked at you in that way, you saw yourself for what you were, reduced to your true dimensions. It was impossible to play-act in front of him, to show off what a good little revolutionary you were. You would start talking straight, and Che would listen to you seriously, wrinkling his forehead and for ever chewing a cigar. And as he watched your face carefully, with just a touch of irony in his big almond-shaped eyes, you would feel the need to select your words with care and to express yourself soberly.

I am trying not to give a bird's eye view of history by describing my personal impression of one man; but after all, history is made by men and it is only human beings who retain impressions which they can transmit. And Che, who is now becoming a folk legend, was first and foremost a man, a man of the next century, a man of the future, an authentic communist who kept us from losing all hope. Che has really lived; while Che continues to live in our minds and to help us all become better, outdo ourselves, all is still possible.

ANIA FRANCOS (France)

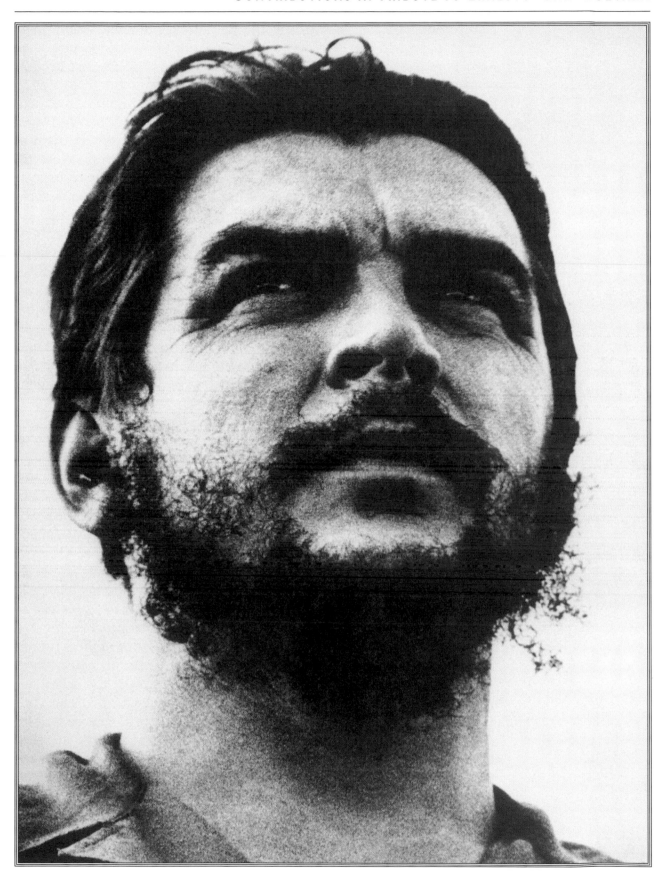

I am writing to you, comrade from a faraway continent, where men aren't happy. We suffer from working and not knowing for whom or why; from producing things that are only measured in terms of money or comfort; from being occupied eight to nine hours a day in exchange for a salary that, no matter how high it is, will never make up for the monotony of our work. We suffer from not being able to contribute, seventeen hours a day, the best of ourselves in exchange only for the happiness of testing the limit of our strength in the common battle against all that degrades mankind, and the happiness of seeing – both in the look of our comrades and in the mark of our imprint on the struggle to be equal, each one for all – that world which is about to be made.

I am writing to you, comrade, from a faraway continent, to tell you that we envy you. You have confirmed what we knew without recognising it; that the only fatherland of the revolutionary is the revolution; that love of liberty must turn into implacable hatred against all those who confuse freedom with their own self interest; that socialism is the negation of money, of commercial relations and of the straight division of labour; that each man can be saved and that he makes history from the moment he triumphs, even for one instant and losing his life in the process, over the forces of inhumanity which still dominate the world.

I am writing to you, comrade, from a faraway continent, to tell you that from the moment a man like you is bold enough to appear, he discovers and reveals to others that he is not alone but one of hundreds, perhaps thousands, with new and invincible ideas. I, who am not a Christian, am telling you that your assassins suffer from the same illusions as the Romans, who one thousand nine hundred and thirty years ago, executed, next to two bandits, a Jewish agitator who had not got with him more than a dozen men; his ideas have triumphed all the same over the imperial state which then dominated the world. That will happen to you too, comrade, because it must be so. But it saddens me that you should not see that day; I am saddened not for you, who took the idea of death lightly and considered yourself absolutely replaceable, but for all of us on whom falls the terrible and difficult privilege of outliving you.

ANDRE GORZ (France)

The death of Che Guevara brought a sense of grief and disappointment to people who had no Marxist sympathies. He represented the idea of gallantry, chivalry and adventure in a world more and more given up to business arrangements between the great world powers; he expressed for us the hope that victory did not always go to the big battalions. One found among the most conservative a genuine sorrow that numbers and weapons had won again, and that

Opposite: Che Guevara reading after the early days of victory.

the adventure of the twelve in Cuba had not been repeated. Was this the end of the forlorn hope, the fight against odds? But the circumstances of Che's death begin to give us comfort. That he was shot after capture demonstrates the fear that the Bolivian authorities felt even of an imprisoned Che. They were afraid to bring him to trial: afraid of the echoes his voice would have aroused from the courtroom: afraid to prove that the man they hated was loved by the world outside. This fear will help to perpetuate his legend, and a legend is impervious to bullets.

GRAHAM GREENE (England)

Not because you've fallen
does your light shine less brightly.
Your guerrilla's silhouette
sits astride a horse of fire
between the wind and clouds of the Sierra.
You are not silent although they've hushed you up.
And although they burn you,
although they hide you underground,
although they conceal you
in cemeteries, forests, mountains,
they won't stop us from finding you,
Che Comandante,
friend.

NICHOLAS GUILLEN (Cuba)

Little soldier of Bolivia,
Little Bolivian soldier,
you go armed with your rifle,
which is an American rifle,
which is an American rifle,
little soldier of Bolivia,
which is an American rifle.

It was given to you by Señor Barrientos,
little Bolivian soldier,
a present from Mister Johnson
to kill your brother,
to kill your brother,
little soldier of Bolivia,
to kill your brother.

You don't know who is the dead man?
little Bolivian soldier?
The dead man is Che Guevara,
and he was Argentine and Cuban,
and he was Argentine and Cuban,
little soldier of Bolivia,
and he was Argentine and Cuban.

He was your best friend,
little Bolivian soldier,
he was the friend of the poor
from the oriente to the altiplano
from the oriente to the altiplano
little soldier of Bolivia
from the oriente to the altiplano

The whole of my guitar
little Bolivian soldier,
is in mourning, but not crying,
though to cry is human,
though to cry is human,
little soldier of Bolivia,
though to cry is human.

This is no time to cry
little Bolivian soldier,
we need no tears nor hankies
but a machete in the hand,
but a machete in the hand,
little soldier of Bolivia,
but a machete in the hand.

With the coppers that they pay you,
little Bolivian soldier,
they sell you and they buy you
that's what the tyrants think,
that's what the tyrants think,
little soldier of Bolivia,
that's what the tyrants think.

Wake up the time has come,
little Bolivian soldier,
and all the world sits up,
because the sun has risen early,
because the sun has risen early,

little soldier of Bolivia,
because the sun has risen early.

Take the right road,
little Bolivian soldier,
it isn't always the easy road,
it isn't always easy or smooth,
it isn't always easy or smooth,
little soldier of Bolivia,
it isn't always easy or smooth.

But you are bound to learn
little Bolivian soldier,
that a brother must not be killed
that you mustn't kill a brother,
that you mustn't kill a brother,
little soldier of Bolivia,
that you mustn't kill a brother.

NICHOLAS GUILLEN (Cuba)

The cause of Fidel and Che has become the cause of all future communism, the kind of communism which has never been put into practise anywhere and which would perhaps do well not to call itself communism while it forges a new method of combat more in keeping with the new situation in which we find ourselves. The history of the Cuban Revolution clearly shows what we can already hope for in the future: to stop dwelling obsessively on the events and difficulties of the past, and to stimulate the trust, imagination and initiative of everyone in every walk of life.

The ever-growing interest that European intellectuals feel in the Third World is not, as some might believe, merely 'escapism' nor a romantic delusion which has no connection with the problems confronting them. It is the bourgeoisie (along with a few so-called left-wingers who don't realise that they are repeating all the bourgeois slogans) which would like to pass off Régis Debray as a new Lord Byron whose wish to do good is both naïve and old-fashioned. It is also the bourgeoisie which would like to compare El Che to Jesus Christ in order to vitiate the political significance of his ideas and his life.

In fact, authentic revolutionary European intellectuals are internationalists like all other authentic revolutionaries everywhere else. These revolutionary intellectuals of Europe are aware of the fact that their battles cannot be waged on the same level as in Latin

CHE

1959 1969 Décimo aniversario del triunfo de la rebelión cubana
Dixiéme anniversaire du triomphe de la rébellion cubaine 1959 1969
1959 1969 Tenth anniversary of the triumph of the Cuban rebellion

21 22

tricontinental

tricontinental

tricontinental

10 tricontinental

tricontinental

TRICONTINENTAL
25

Carta del Che leída por Fidel

En cualquier lugar que nos sorprenda la muerte, bienvenida sea, siempre que ése, nuestro grito de guerra, haya llegado hasta un oído receptivo, y otra mano se tienda para empuñar nuestras armas, y otros hombres se apresten a entonar los cantos luctuosos con tableteo de ametralladoras y nuevos gritos de guerra y de victoria.

¡HASTA LA VICTORIA SIEMPRE!

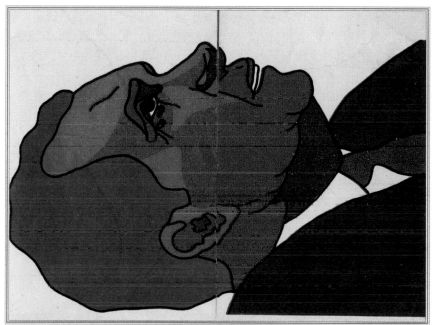

Nixon shows his fangs in this unfolding cartoon, printed in 1968 in Havana.

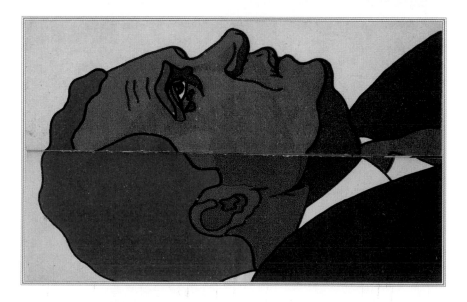

BRISONS
LES VIEUX ENGRENAGES

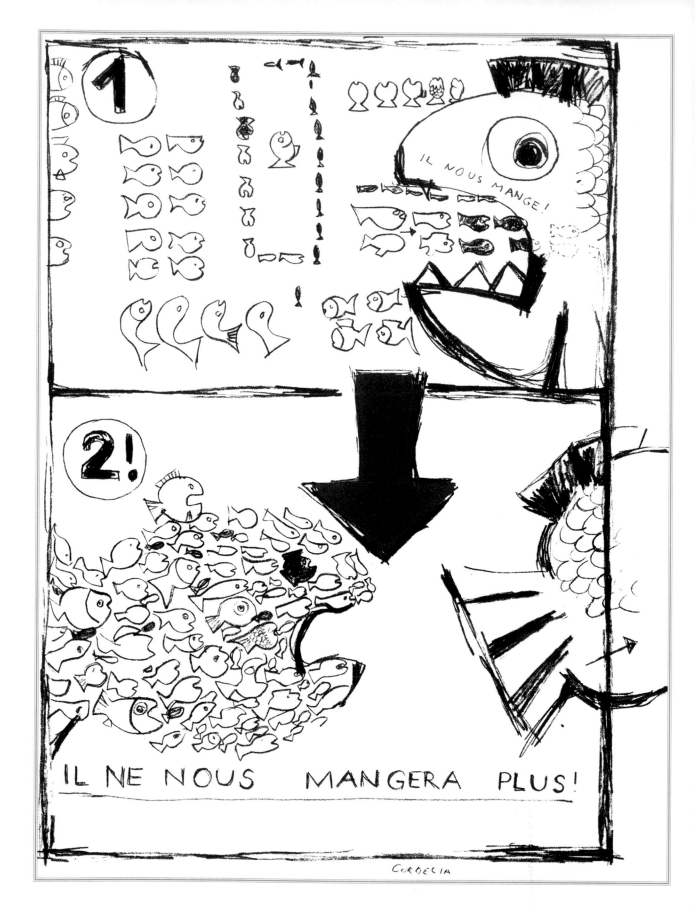

AVEC LES ÉTUDIANTS CONTRE

LA CHIENLIT C'EST LUI!

ÉCOLE Nle SUPÉRIEURE
DES BEAUX-ARTS
17, Quai Malaquais - VIe

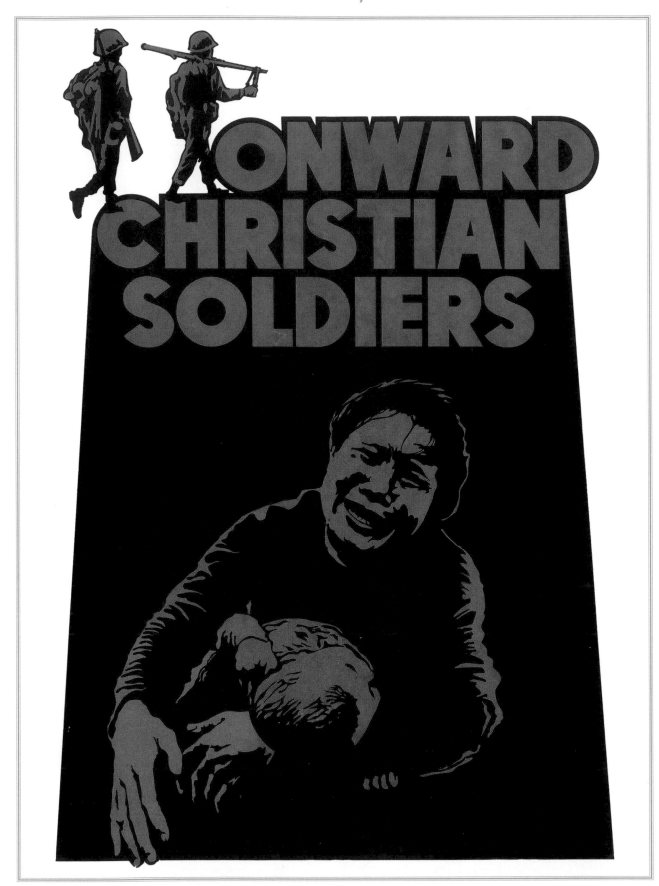

RETALIATION TO CRIME: REVOLUTIONARY VIOLENCE
RÉPONSE AU CRIME: LA VIOLENCE RÉVOLUTIONNAIRE
RESPUESTA AL ASESINATO: VIOLENCIA REVOLUCIONARIA

الرد على العنف الثوري   رداصل الجريمة!!

America, and this is the major issue which they have to resolve. For obviously ideas cannot have the same impact on industrialised nations as on underdeveloped ones. Words as well as attitudes have to be adapted to different circumstances. But European intellectuals do follow the progress of the revolutionary struggles in the Third World with tremendous attention. For that is the only way in which they can define their own attitudes both towards society and for themselves.

It is largely thanks to the Third World that European intellectuals have been able to discover today who they are, what they want and why they want it. The revolutionary individual within a capitalistic society is like a Third World all of his own: his particular tactics must be like those of a guerrilla fighter, always changing terrain and breaking out of the official cultural channels which try to encircle him. A cultural revolution is taking place in China; tomorrow, we could have a cultural guerrilla war all over Europe. I think this would be a good thing because it might then lead to the emergence of a new culture which would eventually give birth to the New Man Che Guevara spoke about: the individual in a state of permanent revolt.

ALAIN JOUFFROY (France)

Week of Che Guevara, hunted, hurt,
held prisoner one lost day, then gangstered down
for gold, for justice – violence cracking on violence,
like rock on rock, the corpse of the last armed prophet
laid out on a sink in a shed, displayed by flashlight –
as the leaves light up, still green, this afternoon,
and burn to balding reds; as the oak, lop-branched
to go on living, swells with goitres like a fruit-tree,
as the walls of the high white stone buildings over-
awe the poor, too good for this new world,
this New York, where our clasped, illicit hands
pulse, stop the bloodstream, as if it hit rock . . .
Rest them for the outlaw . . . kings once hid in oaks,
with prices on their heads, and watched for game.

(This is what it is, and no more a tribute to Che than Shakespeare's Hotspur is a tribute.)

ROBERT LOWELL (USA)

Haiku for Che

December. Late birds shake their wings.
On the snowy windscreen of a car, I write
CHE LIVES!

CHRISTOPHER LOGUE (England)

The revolutionary
Believed in revolution —
Even in art. What was real
Was too good for 'realism'. Burn
L'art pompier! Such a smell
As those waxworks flared, and their glass
Eyes dropped from the sockets and rolled
On the floor, gleefully winking.
Only what was alive would do.

Yet he died, and the photograph
His enemies took of him showed
A face that looked like wax. He lay
There on the rough boards – a dummy
Which even resemblance had left.

The thing is, one shouldn't accept
What one's enemies make of one.
They killed you, Che. But your mind lives,
And it speaks as plainly. No wax
For you, no frozen heroic
Poses. Merely a name which now
When we speak it, honours mankind.

EDWARD LUCIE-SMITH (England)

When this great dishonour looming over Latin America is paid for,
When this great shame is washed away with the good soap made from the blood
    of heroes,
When freedom no longer means wads of dollars and deceit,
Then comrades you'll see how a phoenix rises from its ashes,
And it doesn't matter if the same sun which shines now on the tomb
of the fallen guerrilla
Shines on the sterile sword of the sad sad generals.

Man, why this anger, woman, why these tears?
Don't you know that a hero must die, and that the beautiful wind must blow him away?
The hero had a message too urgent to wait,
and a watchfulness too full of protest,
In other words an irritating menace and a nuisance.
Which is why when the hero falls the wicked rejoice full face,
while the wary common people ache in profile.
Oh, Che, you won't see me weeping over your defeated flesh,
Because yet again I look at the scales where the balance of your last battle is weighed;
And looking at these scales I can say to your enemies and ours:
'You have turned a fallible guerrilla into an infallible force,
And that force which cannot falter is coming to life in Santa Cruz,
And is already setting the rhythm of future battles.'

LEOPOLD MARECHAL (Argentina)

Che's Tale

Che once told the story
Of how during a fight
A man called for silence
'Without knowing why,'
        (was Che's comment)

It's now become a legend
That in this continent
People shouldn't remain silent

Which is why El Che,
Gun smoking in his hand
His finger on the trigger,
To the Andes went . . .
        (and now is silent)

MANUEL DIAZ MARTINEZ (Cuba)

An Impersonal Note to Che Guevara

I don't know what you were like.
I've looked at the photos,
Read what Fidel had to say,
Gone through your books, speeches.

I've got a feeling that if I'd met you,
I might have found you arrogant, or mad.
So what I say about you is not personal,
Nor do I want to be you, now or later.

I just want to say that my mind is richer for your thoughts,
My humanity prouder for your actions,
My life less acceptable for your death,
My death more acceptable for your life.

JOHN MCGRATH (England)

Anyone who has experienced the Cuban Revolution at first hand, who has talked with workers and peasants and their revolutionary leaders, must have been nauseated by the vicious column in the *Daily Mail* written by Bernard Levin at the time of 'Che' Guevara's death. One would not normally waste time on the hysterical and ignorant rubbish which pours from Levin's pen when he contemplates the 'undemocratic' regime of Castro, and the 'murderous' and 'terroristic' activities of Guevara. However, Levin also vented a certain amount of spleen on what he described as 'the fools in the West . . .' who support the Cuban Revolution and admired Guevara. Behind his choleric emotions, cheapness of language, and indifference to rational anaysis, Levin speaks no doubt for the 'wise.' For those, that is to say, who cannot stomach violent revolution in the first place and who believe in any case that a revolutionary government will turn out to be as vile, if not more so, than the tyranny it has overthrown.

There are chilling precedents which superficially justify this conviction – but the case of Cuba, and the meaning of Guevara, deserve more careful examination. If there is to be revolutionary conflict in Latin America and elsewhere in the second half of this century – and this is virtually certain – we cannot afford the luxury of liberal denunciation, but must analyse the actual historical processes leading to death, violence and terror. We cannot afford a morality unilluminated by a profound understanding of the conditions in which men are prepared to fight and die rather than subsist in a 'peace' which keeps them economically and spiritually on their knees. The subtleties and dilemmas of intellectuals who operate from a comfortable distance, and in the comfort of materially advanced societies, become nothing more than a kind of historical voyeurism. The 'fools in the West' at least recognise this, and conclude that a political philosophy and morality which will not come to terms with the necessary overthrow of capitalist penetration and domination in the Third World, is sterile. But the foolish and the wise alike may find themselves, in the coming upheavals, as irrelevant as

Che Guevara on a Havana bus,
known as the gua-gua.

the ladies who took their picnic baskets to the Crimean heights to watch a battle or two in civilized security.

There has been without doubt a certain amount of myth-making about Guevara in the West and elsewhere. This is not to say that Che was anything less than his legend, but rather that his combination of revolutionary idealism and concrete action have had a considerable impact on the scepticism which has perniciously undermined engaged opinion throughout the world. In so far as he was an exponent of violence, it was a counter-violence to that of entrenched reactionary authority whose crimes, tortures and suppressions of popular resistance in Latin America are beyond question. Of course, the violence of the revolution is 'terrorism' by Western terms of reference. For every statistic of fascist savagery, there seems to be an equally horrifying statitistic of revolutionary terror to cancel it out – as if human suffering were explicable in some sort of ideological profit and loss account. Peasants in the Sierra Maestra and workers in the Cuban towns required no indoctrination to understand that nothing short of violent opposition would put an end to the Batista regime. What is more, they came to realise in the course of their struggle – a discovery shared by Castro and Guevara – that simply to eliminate the Batista regime would not be enough. Their needs determined their social objectives, and their needs required the termination of the colonial status of Cuba *vis-à-vis* the USA.

Once this had been achieved, Guevara felt compelled to move on – to carry the struggle, and his analysis of his Cuban experience, onto the main continent. It is natural for those who feel helpless in Europe to identify with the potent image of an intellectual, a humanist and a fighter whose actions are consistent with his words. We do not make history, we are insulated from it – trapped in our lives, our culture, and the sickening momentum of technological transformation which throws up nothing human and offers only a kind of pseudo-liberation for privileged individuals. Most people work and live and die much as they always have, except in greater material comfort. Vision has sunk to the horizons of politicians and technocrats, of managers and education-factories. The meagre liberation of the few is into the almost narcissistic recognition of their paralysis, failure, apathy – and even understanding and insight seem to lead finally to an agonised shrug or a hysterical shout.

But Guevara's life is a reminder of what is possible, of what is being done. We are closing up for what may be the last and most implacable confrontation of all – that between the humiliated poor and the arrogant rich, on an international scale. Nothing short of revolution will overcome underdevelopment, yet what will overcome the armed hostility of the USA and the West in general, to revolution? And will the Soviet Union continue to hover uncertainly between the turbulence in Asia and Latin America, and the bigoted ferocity in Washington? Are we to see these historical contradictions through the eyes of Che Guevara, or simply with the compassionate yet abdicating resignation of people accustomed to understanding much and doing little?

The significance of Che is not a solution but a question.

DAVID MERCER (England)

Letters to Che: Canto Bilingue

Te escribo cartas, Che,
En la sazon de lluvias
Envenenadas

They came without faces
Found you with eyeless rays
The tin grasshoppers
With five-cornered magic
Wanting to feed you
To the man-eating computer

Te escribo cartas, Guerrero,
Vestido de hojas y lunas

But you won and became
The rarest jungle tree
A lost leopard
Out of metal's way

Te escribo cartas
Hermano invisible
Gato de la noche lejana

Cat of far nights
Whisper of a Bolivian kettle
Cry
Of an Inca hill

Te escribo cartas, Niño
De la musica callada.

THOMAS MERTON (USA)

How to Kill Cuba

You must burn the people first.
Then the grass and trees, then the stones.
You must cut the island out of all the maps,
The history books, out of the old newspapers,
Even the newspapers which hated Cuba,

And burn all these, and burn
The paintings, poems and photographs and films
And when you have burnt all these
You must bury the ashes
You must guard the grave
And even then
Cuba will only be dead like Che Guevara —
Technically dead, that's all,
Technically dead.

ADRIAN MITCHELL (England)

The way he lived and died is a saga, of the twentieth century. It tells me: Whatever things we fight for ultimately become, they are worth dying for. Those who give their life for these things will remain forever a testimony of man's need to overcome his own nature, his own destiny. Without men like Che there would be no more hope left. I believe he knew he would die, but I also feel that death for him was more acceptable than the inevitable compromises a victorious revolution always leads to. A revolution is clean, while it fights against odds. Che wanted to remain clean and has remained so. If there were thousands of Ches, those who make life on earth a misery would probably get scared and leave us in peace. There must be thousands of Ches if we want to survive with dignity.

JIRI MUCHA (Czechoslovakia)

What can I say about Che that has not already been said?
That I remember the night when I got to know him by the light of the fires.
That at one time we were enemies, but in spite of that, I admired him.
That afterwards I asked to work especially with him. And one day I put my hand on his shoulder as a sign of affection and he said to me: Is that trust? And my hand fell.
The days passed and one day he said to me: Do you know? You are

Opposite: Che Guevara playing chess, one of his favourite games.

not such a bastard as they told me you were. And we laughed and became friends.

What can I say about Che that has not already been said?

That one day I asked him: Haven't you ever known fear? and he answered: A terrible fear.

That in the most sectarian days, an extremist attacked the 26th of July movement, and after thinking about it I said to Che: It is true that we knew nothing about Marxism and we did not belong to the party; but perhaps thanks to that, we were able to pull down Batista.

And we talked things over.

That when I was at my most anti-sectarian and unjustly attacked some old communist, Che told me off.

That once, when someone criticised the shortage of food, he said that it was not true, that in his home they ate reasonably well.

Perhaps you receive an additional quota, I said to him, half-seriously and half-jokingly.

Later he called us to tell us: 'It was true, until yesterday we were getting an additional quota.'

What can I say about Che that has not already been said?

That I remember the early mornings in the Ministry of Industry when we used to joke while waiting for the time to leave for our voluntary work. He used to come at night to Juceplán and after the exhausting meetings he used to play a game of chess with the guards, while we sat round them singing softly, and out of tune, old tangos of his childhood.

That at the beginning he was very strict in the matter of women but ended up by saying that he didn't look after the fly of anybody else's trousers.

That I remember the night when my mother died, when we were not yet real friends, and those who were friends did not come to see me. I remember, I repeat, he arrived at dawn for the funeral and he put his hand on my shoulder, as I had done to him that other time. And he stayed talking to me for hours until it was daytime.

That afterwards, when I no longer worked with him, and went on wishing to see him, each time I went to his office we would talk interminably. Manresa would ask for coffee. Che would throw himself on the floor, on the carpet, smoking. When the air-conditioner broke down, we would open the windows and take our shirts off. We settled the world then. Well, look here, little polack, he would say.

But we were old night-birds and I would not leave until dawn was breaking, and we would go down together in the elevator, he complaining that I made him waste a lot of time.

What can I say about Che that has not already been said?

That I have not yet been able to pluck up courage to go and see Aleida and have a look at the kids.

Opposite: Che Guevara at a banquet.

That when I saw the photographs of Bolivia, he lying on the dais, with his naked body, I remembered the nights when he lay on the carpet in his office, in the Ministry of Industry, with a look that went beyond all things, with a brightness in his eyes like a reflection of the stars, the stars of the South.

What can I say?

ENRIQUE OLTUSKI (Cuba)

GUEVARA IS DEAD . . . LONG LIVE GUEVARA!

'There is no definition of socialism which makes sense for us,' said Che Guevara, 'but the abolition of exploitation of one man by another.' Or of one country by another. The West is Billy Bunter in a world of Oliver Twists and Guevara saw no boundaries; for exploiters are running free in Athens and Djakarta, Saigon and the Congo. So he taught tin miners to throw dynamite, mountain Indians to use their traps for war. The Doctor took up a carbine (yet lagged behind the guerrilla bands of the Cuban Revolution to care for the wounded on both sides). Men like Guevara are too big and angry for our world of typewriters and soft hands; too big for the courtroom of Camiri, too honest for those fat men in the Kremlin who ordered their parties to betray the guerrillas and whose revolution goes on in drapes and velours, and too serious to live into middle age.

OZ MAGAZINE (England)

The death of Jack Kennedy was painful to intellectuals less because they admired him than because they believed that he admired them. Guevara's death is not painful in this sense; no intelligent person living in an advanced country except in a state of total dissent (and how many can achieve or sustain that condition?) can fail to realise, without grievous self-deception, that he is, by the very fact of his comfortable existence, someone whom Guevara would not have admired, whom Guevara accuses. Guevara's death may create a myth; it also removes a critic. . . .

No question about it. I am not fighting for the starving or the oppressed except, fitfully, with words, guiltily, patronisingly, with gifts. I am as inclined as most to fall into the ritual posture of stagey solidarity when faced with Guevara's example. He makes Verkhovenskys of us all. Make no mistake: I do not especially blame myself. Objectively, it is impossible to do right in the present world situation so long as one accepts (by one's life, not one's words) the divisions of rich and poor. We literally owe the world to the destitute and the oppressed, who still compose the vast majority, and Guevara, who was both an educated man (education being itself almost a reproach and yet the only hope) and a completely dispossessed person, demonstrated the possibility of a bridge between the two irreconcilables of rich and poor. The assumption that the problem is too big for individual action reveals the degree of alienation from which we now suffer. We, the important, rule ourselves out as serious contributors to the world struggle and leave it to the poor to be real. As Wittgenstein endlessly pointed out, nothing can be true in the world unless it is possible for it also to be false; the saying can be reversed: we are in the situation of scarcely even being able meaningfully to be false, since there is scarcely any sense in which we can be true. Guevara is almost meaningless to us as an example: in the global village, everything is happening at the other end of town and, if we are honest about our reactions, we thank our gods for it.

FREDERIC RAPHAEL (USA)

In Cuba the image of Che Guevara is everywhere, on gigantic posters and postage stamps, in offices and shops, in books and periodicals of every kind. Che, a guerrilla leader and hero in his lifetime, has become by virtue of his tragic death, a martyr and secular saint.

From Cuba this hero-worship spreads throughout Central and South America. Even in Puerto Rico, dominated as it is by American capital and propaganda, the image of Che appears surreptitiously on lamp-posts and hoardings.

For the first time in its history the communist movement has found a romantic hero, a hero in the tradition of Count Roland or the Black Prince; a political hero as charismatic as Mickiewicz or Garibaldi. But to the people of Latin America he is more than any hero of the past. He is the ideal human being, physically beautiful, morally clean, and politically incorruptible.

The last hero remotely comparable to Che was Lawrence of Arabia, but Lawrence was an ambiguous figure – sexually ambiguous and politically indecisive. Che was a happily married man with five children and his political ideals were precise and precisely formulated. He had style, in his life and actions, in his thought and writing. He was gay and affectionate, and his love embraced the poor and oppressed of the whole world.

When the Revolution triumphed in Cuba and he could look forward to a life of comparative ease and power, he renounced it. The Revolution could not end in Cuba; it must be carried to Cuba's neighbouring peoples, to every country where the working classes were enslaved and exploited.

Impossible to doubt Che's idealism; impossible not to admire his courage and self-sacrifice.

But it is legitimate to express doubts about his methods, his revolutionary strategy. Moral doubts and political doubts.

Che Guevara believed in the necessity of violence to achieve his revolutionary aims. I am a pacifist and believe that violence is morally wrong and politically inexpedient.

Castro's and Che's tactics of violence were successful in Cuba, but the more one learns about what happened in Cuba nine years ago, the more evident becomes the element of pure chance that ensured a victory for those tactics. Batista's régime was so corrupt that it was ready to crumble at the first appearance of a popular uprising. The United States was caught napping and was not able to crush the Revolution before Castro had secured the active support of Russia. The Bay of Pigs episode was a clumsy fiasco, and the subsequent 'missile crisis' only served to reveal the impotence of the two giants armed with their obliterative bombs.

Since that confrontation the Cuban Revolution has sheltered under the missile umbrella. The United States has tried to destroy the Revolution by other means, by diplomatic intrigues and savage economic sanctions. But Cuba so far has survived and with every month that passes her political position becomes stronger. Her economic position is still precarious, but provided she is not deserted by the rest of the communist world, she will survive. The social and cultural achievements of the régime are already very impressive, which is another cause for the resentment of her enemies.

The missile umbrella is very relevant to the whole question of guerrilla tactics. Che had a pathetic faith in these tactics; so had the majority of the delegates who assembled in Havana for the recent Cultural Congress. But what happened to Che in Bolivia is an illustration of the futility of these tactics. Apart from the fact that they can be employed only under the shelter of the missile umbrella (for one 'strategic weapon' would wipe out any isolated guerrilla action), these tactics depend on the myth of a co-operative peasantry. But everything, even in the Cuban Revolution, goes to show that the peasantry is the most indifferent and even hostile class in a revolutionary situation. The peasant with his three acres and a cow, or whatever may be the regional equivalent, is not militant by nature nor upbringing. He is rooted to the earth and makes a most indifferent activist. I was told in Havana that in Bolivia Che had succeeded in enlisting from the Bolivian countryside only ten peasants. Of these, two had defected and one had betrayed him.

Guerrilla warfare, as a revolutionary strategy, is a romantic myth. In the modern world, even in 'underdeveloped' countries, the only realistic strategy is the general strike of industrial workers. The peasants can hold up food supplies, but that takes months to be effective. The industrial workers – transport, electrical, distributive, sanitary – can paralyse a community in twenty-four hours. Such is a non-violent strategy of revolution, and in all but freak circumstances it is the only strategy.

But there is something more to Che than his romantic reliance on violence. He was above all a humanist, and believed that it was possible to create a 'new man'. Society must be 'a huge school', he said, and he saw the new man beginning to emerge in the period of the building of socialism. 'His image is as yet unfinished; in fact it will never be finished, since the process advances parallel to the development of new economic forms.' But the process was not to be one of brain-washing, of mass propaganda – 'the individual receives the impact of the new social power and perceives that he is not completely adequate to it. Under the influence of the pressure implied in indirect education, he tries to adjust to a situation that he feels to be just and whose lack of development has kept him from doing so thus far. He is educating himself.' As far as the masses are concerned, Che recognised that it would be a long and difficult road, and man can only advance along that road if he breaks the chains of alienation. 'This will be translated concretely into the reappropriation of his nature through freed work and the expression of his own human condition in culture and art.'

There seems to be no doubt that Che Guevara was responsible for the exceptional degree of intellectual and artistic freedom that prevails in Cuba – for the deliberate rejection of a socialist realism based on the bourgeois art of the last century, and the inauguration of a new art worthy of the new man. 'It is the 21st Century man we must create, although this is still a subjective and not a realised aspiration. It is not a question of how many kilograms of meat are eaten or how many times a year someone may go on holiday to the sea shore or how many pretty imported things can be bought with present wages. It is rather that the individual feels greater fulfilment, that he has greater inner wealth and many more responsibilities. In our country the individual knows that the glorious period in which it has fallen to him to live is one of sacrifice; he is familiar with sacrifice.'*

It is this emphasis on individualism, found in Castro as well as in Che Guevara, that makes the Cuban Revolution so distinctive and so different from the doctrinaire régimes of the USSR and Eastern Europe. There was nothing dogmatic about Che. He believed that, 'We

* *These quotations come from* Man and Socialism in Cuba, *a translation of* El Socialismo y el Hombre en Cuba *(1965) published by the Book Institute in Havana in 1967.*

socialists are more free because we are more fulfilled; we are more fulfilled because we are more free.' His great appeal is based on this spirit of freedom and sacrifice. He also dared to use the word 'love'. 'The true revolutionary,' he pointed out, 'is guided by strong feelings of love. Our vanguard revolutionaries must idealise this love for the peoples, for the most hallowed causes, and make it one and indivisible.'

It would be self-deception to present Che as a libertarian socialist, but in everything he said and did he was nearer to the spirit of Kropotkin and Tolstoy than to that of Lenin and Stalin. Even the stage of guerrilla warfare (and he described it as a 'stage') was seen as 'a catalyst which created the subjective condition necessary for victory.' But 'the individual was also the basic factory in the guerrilla, in the framework of the gradualisation of our thinking, in the revolution taking place in our habits and in our minds.' Without that personal heroism, that individual sense of glory, nothing would have been achieved in Cuba.

HERBERT READ

El Commandante

So they shot at this left leg with which I'd walked
all over the world; not even a tree
to tell them off, and vipers, vipers
that hiss like bullets: catch him! crush him!
And the asthma too and one other thing,
so that makes three. The asthma, the asthma. . . .

So that makes three or three o'clock,
and it isn't October and it isn't the eighth,
and that is the way the ravine ends,
the Yuro ravine, and that is the way
the ravine of the world bursts open
and closes over. In October they shot me.

Five thousand dollars (or was it fifty?)
for this blood of mine, and was it for this
that we were and are? They gave five thousand
for my eyes and hands, fifty thousand the lot!
with the asthma thrown in, the bad lungs too,
that were going to sing my fortieth birthday.

The fatal whine of death's mosquitos
sing 'Up with the poor! *Arriba*! Fire!'
Flash of machine-guns, welcome the bullets
if others come after. Quick! let's run
Quick, oh quick, to avenge the dead man.

Mine, what's mine? This rose, this America,
with all its odd thorns. All that dawn
they judged me in English. What's mine is mine,
and yours too, brother. What a blow!
straight in the heart where fear begins.

And so they bled me, then they burnt me,
in Vallegrande — and took me there
in a helicopter — there's nothing wrong
with sprinkling blood to refresh the air,
even though after that they burnt my body,
chopped off both hands: Go on, shoot! Don't stop!

I'll be back, Bolivar, but now I'm off. . . .

GONZALO ROJAS (Chile)

The tense voice of Fernández Retamar sounds and resounds in our
ears. In the aeroplane that took us from Mexico to Havana in March,
1967, he was singing

> Here remains the clear
> intimate transparence
> of your dear presence
> Comandante Che Guevara.

We did not know where the verses or the music came from
although some of us noted that from their grace and love, they were
of Cuban origin. In no other country than Cuba could that quartet
have been written or sung, for there that presence of intimate
transparency lives with such force.

That was in March. We are now in October. And now that clarity
and that transparency, which the Cuban poet was praising, is not only
in Cuba. It has extended to all America. The obscene military hand
that murdered the man in Vallegrande, did not know how much it
was making that presence grow, that clarity, that transparence. The
Gorillas of America will disappear in obscurity, sunk in their own
abjection or in that of their masters. They will disappear like opaque
and dirty shadows.

Che Guevara making a speech to the Cuban people.

109

Ernesto Guevara – 'veteran and guerrilla' as his brother Fidel called him – will become each day more clear, more transparent and more engraved in our hearts and in the land of America.

For all and for ever, glorious and sorrowful; and now I would like to sing in memory of him, with my bad voice the song I heard Fernández Retamar sing: but I cannot. No one can sing in mourning no matter how much clarity there is, and I do not know if I could again.

MANUEL ROJAS (Chile)

The Bee Hive

I don't believe in ghosts
yet surgeons transplant a living heart
into the chest cavity of a dead man
a fisty pulping orange
. . . a new ticker !

But for a bullet hole in the heart
there is no second valentine for a Marxist.
The worms have murdered the tiger. Che is dead.
And in time, we too shall face the bee keeper
for they who move with tender feet
through the saw-mills of the hive
they shall hear a hymn of Carpenter bees
whose furnace song is dum-dum's liturgy.

In secret ground they've buried Che's dust
trembling like monks who hide religious radium
from the lead eyes of the poor.

J. ROSENBLATT (Canada)

Che Guevara interests me as a writer, as a thinker and as a man of action. To know him, you have to read what he wrote as well as find out the details of his life. Not only were his ideas great ideas; they also had, first and foremost, the coherence of ideas which had been put into practice as well as preached by a man who finally sacrificed his life for them.

Che was not dogmatic, nor was he a demagogue, as is so often the case in the realm of ideas. The very way in which he expressed himself was characteristic: he would speak as though he were seeking a truth within himself that he was trying to communicate to others.

Che Guevara on Cuban radio.

Many intellectuals like myself have splendid ideas, but not all intellectuals have either the moral strength or the physical courage to put their ideas into practice. Che Guevara had this strength and that is why he will go down in history as a great man. He was the link between the Cuban Revolution in action and the revolution over the whole Latin American continent. Cuba can justly feel proud of Che's internationalism, which was the living embodiment of the revolutionary doctrine.

Some ideas are greater than men, but some men are as great as their ideas. I don't just say this because I believe it is true, but because Che Guevara has proved that it is true.

FRANCESCO ROSI (Italy)

EPITAPH TO BE PLACED ON A MAP OF AMERICA

Here lies Ernesto Guevara; they buried him in a box of earth and fear and they covered it up with the skyless night of the forest.

This tomb is in the jagged shape of a map of America : it is trodden by the bare feet of those who bear the shackles of poverty round their ankles and who wear the truth like a grimy halo.

He was a hero and an artist, because an artist is a man who transcends his creation, and a hero's work of art is that last gesture of his life in which he gives up his life in order to kill his death.

At that instant, the idea becomes the ideal, and the ideal then transcends the cold logic of intelligence to attain the mysterious realm of aesthetics; it is there that the ideal becomes one with flesh, becomes one with pain and with fear, and takes on the shape of the act that called it into existence. Thus heroism and art are fused into one and the same thing.

In warfare, Guevara was a humanist; for armed struggle only meant one thing to him : that gesture which America is beginning to make, that gesture of picking up a rifle in battle, a rifle that turns the hand which holds it into a clenched fist.

DALMIRO SAENZ (Argentina)

Che Guevara's life is the finest example of Caribbean-American revolutionary heroism I know; the news of his death, the most humbling and numbing I have experienced, is similar in personal loss to a death in one's own family. His legendary life and tragic death are as much mine, and ours, as they are gloriously his; his life's work and its terrible termination are a revolutionary whole. How acceptable Sartre's rhetoric sounds, now, a matter of months after Che's assassination: '(He) was not only an intellectual but also the most complete human being of our age.'

Che's heroism has many meanings, and each has its unique importance, because each satisfies our particular memory of his exemplary life and death : as Bolívar's historical heir; Fidel's spiritual other self; the New World's avenging vistor; and as the universal symbol of the modern revolution. Above all, there is his definition of solidarity through direct involvement and action, a demand which few are physically and morally able to meet: 'It is not a matter of wishing success to the victim of aggression, but of sharing his fate; one must accompany him to his death or to victory.'

Very nearly all the lessons drawn from Che's revolutionary struggles, beginning with his and Fidel's intensive guerrilla training in Mexico and continuing in combat in Cuba, and later, alone, in Bolivia, have been instructions in armed acts of solidarity, not only to the serving men and women in the hills and in the towns, but also to the intellectuals. The peasants and intellectuals, often recalcitrant and inherently conservative, have been crucial elements in the effective unification of all modern revolutionary movements, as Che has always emphasized. His daunting challenge to the intellectuals to become men of decisive armed action has been uncompromising. His lesson, here, is that ideas must lead to action or they will slide back into dreams, and that, equally urgently, action without the salt of ideology ends as empty action. The natural revolutionary intellectual is always hard to come by, and Che knew it.

He also knew that guerrilla confrontations with a monstrous enemy must be spread over the broadest possible area, with highly sensitive and aggressive focus points, and that the assaults must be militarily and morally humiliating and decisive. Che saw the absurdly lonely figure of David, standing up to Goliath, as an essential factor in David's own spiritual rehabilitation.

In the Caribbean, Latin America and elsewhere throughout the dispossessed world (and this does not exclude certain bruised and declining developed countries), Che believed in liberation at any price for the exploited and dominated, and his Cuban and Bolivian call has been that the dynamic movements of the people in the underdeveloped sectors will create their new leaders who will be avenging and revolutionary; Che was not without the fervour of idealism, tempered as it was with sound, international political good sense.

What does all this mean to me? What did Che's life and death mean in plain, human terms? Each was a lesson in living; each was a definition towards the fuller, richer, independent life; each was tragic and beautiful for me, in the Caribbean, and for me, in Europe and in Asia and Africa. If it is yet possible for those of the revolutionary faith to have hope, may we hope that 'the sad body' will see us gathered, 'all the men on earth', and be 'moved' to leave his death behind and 'walk' with those of us who need him, and with those who think they do not but who do.

ANDREW SALKEY (Jamaica)

Che, where can I write to you? You will tell me where. A miner in Bolivia, a mother in Peru, a guerrilla fighter who may be there now or not, but will be there in the future. I understand all this, Che, because you are the one who taught me and also this letter should not be for you. How can I tell you that I have never cried so much since that night they killed Frank, even though this time I didn't believe it. Everyone was certain, and I said, 'It isn't possible. A bullet can't put an end to what is eternal. You and Fidel have to live on, for if you do not live, how can life go on? In these fourteen years I have seen so many of those I loved dearly die that today I feel weary of life. I feel I have lived too much; the sun is no longer so beautiful; I no longer feel delight when I see the palm tree. At times, like now, though I love life so much that those two things alone make it worth opening my eyes each morning, I wish to have them closed like those others, like you.

How can it be true? This continent does not deserve such a thing. Had your eyes been left open, Latin America would have found her way swiftly. Che, the only thing that could console me is to have gone, too, but I did not go. I am here with Fidel; I have always done what he wished me to do. Do you remember? You promised me in the Sierra; you told me, 'You will not miss coffee, for we shall drink maté.' You had no frontiers, but you promised to call me when you were in your Argentina, and how I waited, since I knew you would make good that promise. Now it cannot be, you were unable, I was unable. Fidel said yes, that it must be true, what sorrow! He could not say 'Che', so he took hold of himself and said 'Ernesto Guevara.' Thus he told the people, your people. What deep sorrow! I cried for the people, for Fidel, for you, because now I could not go. Later, at the memorial ceremony for you, this great people did not know what honours Fidel would bestow on you. The honour was: artist. I had been thinking that no honour would be great enough; all too trifling; and Fidel, as always, found the true honours: everything you created was perfect, but you created a unique being, you created yourself; you demonstrated how the new man is truly possible. All of us then saw that this new man is a reality, because he exists; you are he. What more can I tell you, Che. If only I knew, like you, how to put things. Anyway, you once wrote me: 'I see you have become a literary person and now master syntax. But I confess to you that the way I like you best is the way you were one New Year's Day, with all the stops out and giving off to beat the band. That image of you and that of the Sierra (even our

Che Guevara relaxing with Fidel Castro in 1959.

arguments of those days seem happy memories now) are the ones I keep for my own personal use.' That is why I could never write about you, and I shall always keep the memory.

Ever onward to victory, beloved Che.

HAYDEE SANTAMARIA (Cuba)

You know how much I admire Che Guevara. In fact, I believe that the man was not only an intellectual but also the most complete human being of our age: as a fighter and as a man, as a theoretician who was able to further the cause of revolution by drawing his theories from his personal experience in battle.

JEAN-PAUL SARTRE (France)

Was his death in vain?
The inevitable outcome for a romantic
adventurer whose vision substituted
the impatient clatter of machine gun
bullets for the inevitable unfolding
of the dialectic?

Did he have a chance?

A writer reminds us:

Fidel,
Back in December, 1956, you landed near Niquero
in the Oriente of Cuba with 82 men and a few arms.
Your plan was to ignite an insurrection which would
rid Cuba of Batista in a few weeks. Instead, you
were to wander through fields and forests in the
dark, without real food or water, living on sugar
cane for five days and five nights.
In the depth of this disaster, you were to
announce to the few men still with you : 'The days
of dictatorship are numbered.'

'This man is crazy,' one of them admits he said
to himself.

That man could have been Che.
This is why we will go on.

DANIEL SCHECHTER (USA)

Confused trembling voices will tell us, they are already telling us, that the death of Che Guevara is a useless sacrifice, though a generous one. A desperate act. An explosion, very beautiful but ineffectual, of the romantic revolution. But no – this death is the culmination of a life, of a series of rational decisions. Isn't it rational for a Marxist to plan to transform reality, to change the apparent dark purpose of the world, such as it is and such as is determined by the economic structures and dominant ideologies of imperialism? This death is a political action and it is our duty to clarify and preserve its political significance: its reasons, its causes, its consequences. To learn from this death. To live from this death, fighting.

JORGE SEMPRUN (Spain)

I'm no expert on Guevara, though I have read his book on guerrilla warfare, and many recent articles that have told quite a lot about him – but by no means everything. A great deal is still to come, and poems and plays will be written about him and his life.

Why is this? Guevara was a frail man with certain great and simple ideas. These two qualities made him immortal, and vulnerable. He died young, and to those who killed him he was an outlaw – but a dangerous one. An army was set on him. He carried ideas to Bolivia, a place everyone now says was the wrong one, and I think they are right, but his ideas were never wrong, and his fate was to choose the wrong place so that his ideas would eventually be proved more right than ever. He was not destined to strike up a spectacular Dien Bien Phu in South America and grow renowned as a general, but what he did do, and leave behind him, will turn out to have been just as vital.

Heroes, theoreticians, martyrs, great leaders will come as they are needed in South America, and Che Guevara had some of all these qualities rolled into his own wide personality.

His ideas were young ideas – they will always be young. In some sense he could not bear to grow old. He didn't have it in him to 'form a government' – and who can blame him? One must applaud him for wanting to make revolutions rather than governments – which in most cases distort all memory of them, turn them into pageants of inhuman clockwork action.

From the evidence, one can deduce much. He was frail, but had a great idea to sustain his body through immense hardship. Life in the jungle has the most devastating effect on the physical system. To survive a week is to survive a lifetime. But a body can live on ideas, though the man must be of an extreme toughness and be absolutely human at the same time. A fanatic would not survive.

One cannot talk about Guevara, however, as if one knew him at school. Too many, no doubt, now knew him at school for any such

Che Guevara with Jean-Paul
Sartre and Simone de Beauvoir
during their visit to Cuba.

evidence to be worth much. But I will stake a lot on certain traits of his character being true, without being tempted into the useless fields of hagiography. In any case, Guevara is no myth. There is someone like him in Colombia at the moment. He is a folk hero though, not only for South America, but for all the world, including the United States. One can easily see why, and if there are any who can't, let them draw their curtains and go back to the fire.

ALAN SILLITOE (England)

Put a bullet in his head
Fields are dumb   the earth is dead
Shoot the rebel from behind
Walls are deaf   the roof is blind
Burn his body   pound his flesh
Blood and water dry to ash
Cut his finger from his hand
Print it as his last command

After Zapata
      Lumumba
Nadie y nada

Put a bullet in his head
Fields are marching   earth is red
Shoot the rebel from behind
Walls have ears   the roof a mind
Burn his body   pound his flesh
Blood and water flood the ash
Cut his finger from his hand
Print it as his last command

After Zapata
      Lumumba
      GUEVARA
Viva la tierra

ANDREW SINCLAIR (England)

Ever since my three-month visit to Cuba in the summer of 1960, the Cuban Revolution has been dear to me, and Che, along with Fidel, have been heroes and cherished models. Che seemed especially compelling. One knew of the intensity of his passion for justice, of his

Opposite: Che Guevara speaking to the Cuban people.

heroic participation in the guerrilla struggle in the Sierra Maestra (in which the usual adversity of struggle was compounded by bouts of crippling asthma), and of the qualities of his mind and the developing maturity of his political thinking, as disclosed in his writings and the speeches he delivered between 1959 and 1965. But it was only with his extraordinary letter of April, 1965, to Fidel, renouncing his position in the Cuban government and his Cuban citizenship to participate in revolutionary struggles elsewhere – as we now know, to lead the guerrilla movement in Bolivia – that one began to grasp the full definition that Che had given to the vocation of the revolutionist. 'The duty of every revolutionary is to make the revolution.' Agreed. But what Che demonstrated by his decision of 1965 – which puts everything that he did during his stay in Cuba in a new light, a wider context – is that the revolutionary aspiration must not be enclosed within nationalisms, and ultimately compromised by identification with the interests of separate nation-states.

The shock of Che's death has been tremendous. Apart from a grim sense of the political importance of his loss, I feel a personal grief that will last a long time. Che survives now only in the 'use' that will be made of his life and his death. What will that use be? I don't disdain the impact of Che as a romantic image, especially among newly radicalised youth in the United States and Western Europe; if the glamour of Che's person, the heroism of his life, the pathos of his death, are useful to young people in strengthening their disaffiliation from the life-style of American imperialism and in advancing the development of a revolutionary consciousness, so much the better. Behind the rhetoric and every struggle stands the figure of an exemplary person. Therefore, it's right that not simply the words and deeds of Che count, but the figure of the whole man. Che is the clearest, most unequivocal image of the humanity of the world-wide revolutionary struggle unfolding today. But it is vital not to allow Che, in our memory of him, to become too abstract a figure : the romantic adventurer (like Lord Byron), the noble underdog (like Zapata), the poet-revolutionary (like Martí). What assists in this distortion is, of course, the fact that he has been cut down. Unfortunately, many people find it easier to revere the person of and give assent to the ideas of a revolutionary leader who has been martyred than one who is alive, engaged in struggle, making mistakes, still developing. People find something inherently appealing in Rosa Luxemburg and Karl Liebknecht, in Trotsky, in Abram Leon, Marcel Hic, and Martin Widelin (European Trotskyites killed by the Nazis), in Patrice Lumumba, in Malcolm X, and now in Che. It seems easier to stand with them than with Fidel, with the NLF, with Hugo Blanco in a Peruvian prison, with Stokely and Rap Brown and James Forman. But Che doesn't, because he is dead, become more admirable than Fidel.

The trap of sentimentalism must be avoided. Merely to consign Che to the pantheon of martyrs is too easy. It would be, moreover, a profoundly unpolitical response to his death.

Che must not be allowed to become an inspiring 'beautiful' legend. Far more useful would be to stress his singularity, Che as a controversial figure on the contemporary revolutionary scene. Only by paying particular attention to his words and deeds will we do his life and death justice.

The main importance of Che is not as a singular personality, a humanly exemplary figure of the 'revolutionary' but as a leader – both in active struggle and theoretical articulation – of a specific movement, the Cuban Revolution, the example of which has revitalized radical consciousness in the 1960's. This in itself has been an enormous contribution and no mean feat, after the lengthy period of cynicism about the validity of Marxist goals induced by the traumatic betrayal of the Russian Revolution by Stalinism and by the counter-revolutionary policies of orthodox communist parties wherever potentially revolutionary situations existed, as in France and Italy in 1945–47 or in Latin America in the last fifteen years (not to mention such outright brutal repressions of democratic revolutionary uprisings, as in Spain in 1936, Poland in 1944, East Germany in 1953, and Hungary in 1956). The behaviour of orthodox, Moscow-oriented communist parties throughout the world since the late 1920's has furnished one of the greatest single obstacles to radical thought and action. But through the example of the new revolutionary options emerging outside of Europe and North America in the neo-colonialist countries, the degenerate revolutionary traditions are finally being effectively contested. It is the independent, though still imperfect and emerging, socialist society of Cuba, along with the heroic struggle of the Vietnamese Revolution which, though it has not yet expelled the American aggressors, has already gone a long way towards expunging its Stalinist heritage, which has given most concrete hope for a revalidation of the Marxist revolutionary tradition.

Che's significance is the role he played in this new revolutionary tradition, which directly opposes major developments in Russia in the last thirty years, in the European states since World War II, and in China. For the revolutionary tradition is not something that can be adhered to *en bloc*. The painful lesson that has been learned is that conformist, anti-democratic, and counter-revolutionary movements can and have used revolutionary theory as mere 'ideology', to promote the interests of a given nation-state (either as a bureaucratic élite exercising power within a nominally 'socialist' country, or as a legitimate minority party effectively supporting the status quo in capitalist or neo-colonial countries). Che more than once quoted Lenin's dictum, 'Without a revolutionary theory there is no revolutionary practice.' True enough. But without an effective, active recognition of the internationalism of authentic revolutionary struggle and a genuine substantive commitment to democratic practices, any revolutionary movement or party must decay into a new vehicle of political oppression and buttress a reconstituted class society. Upon these two principles, Che formed the core of his revolutionary theory. On the internatinalism of the revolutionary movement he staked his own life, by the exemplary didactic act of leaving Cuba to engage in struggle in Bolivia. And Che's role in promoting the creation of socialist democracy in Cuba is less well known, but equally important. It was Che, for instance, who dissuaded Fidel early in 1959, after the revolution took power, from disarming the guerrilla movement and forming a regular army; and argued, successfully, for the creation of a nation-wide militia which would entail that the entire populace continued to bear arms. It is Che who is mainly responsible for the liberty for all tendencies in the arts, including thoroughly apolitical and avant-garde ones, which exists in Cuba. This is hardly to say that the Cuban society has completely achieved the aims of socialist democracy and justice; in at least two important respects, the absence of a free press and of an independent judiciary, it has not. Nevertheless, despite these defects and others, Cuba is in some respects the most genuinely democratic country in the world today; and that is in great measure due to Che's leadership. The fact that Cuba is not still further along the road towards socialist democracy may be partly because Che devoted more and more of his attention and leadership to the first question, that of the internationalism of revolutionary struggle.

Che's argument was that the Revolution in Cuba is not worth preserving, indeed it cannot be preserved as a humane democratic socialism, unless it is extended. This is why the Cuban leadership has staked its existence on the spread of revolution to the rest of Latin America. (We know that this argument, eloquently sponsored by Che, was vigorously opposed by the old-line communist party leadership; and that this leadership, under the title of the 'micro-faction' of Annibal Escalante, was brought to trial and condemned quite recently, shortly after the betrayal and death of Che.) This small, precariously located country of six million people could easily have settled for a status quo nationalist 'communism' like Yugoslavia, that threatened nobody – keeping peace with the Soviet Union and arranging an eventual limited accommodation with the United States. Instead, Cuba has chosen to defy, not only the United States with its blockade, its constant threat of invasion, but also to defy Russia, on which it is dependent for economic support, and to dispute with China as well.

This policy, of which Che is reported to be the principal architect, should not altogether surprise us. In its incredible idealism and daring, it is exactly commensurate with the grandiose task which the Cuban Revolution has set itself. In his essay on *Man and Socialism in Cuba*, written in 1965 for a radical magazine in Uruguay while he was travelling in Africa, Che reaffirmed the classical Marxist horizon of socialist revolution – nothing less than the creation of a new man.

'It is the 21st Century man we must create, although this is still a subjective and not a realised aspiration. It is precisely this man of the century who is one of the fundamental objectives of our work. . . .'

Che himself was not, could not be that new man. But what gives his life its ultimate moral authority is his commitment to that goal, which is nothing less than the cause of humanity itself.

SUSAN SONTAG (USA)

Tune for Che

Che, your comrades will create
A hymn for you of love and hate

Your body is their instrument
Of faith and courage and dissent

Keys have been made from all your bones
To play the scale of human groans

Your skin is stretched to make a drum
That plays the beat of fights to come

From your throat they've made a flute
That pleads for those who are still mute

From your lips a whistle calls
Every time a just man falls

Your heart's a bell that rings each time
An unjust man commits a crime

A guitar from your rib-cage
Plays the sorrow of our age

Your sinews have become the strings
That weep each time the guitar sings

Each of your words is now a song
Which has the power to right a wrong

Each deed a note, each note a word
Each word a song that can be heard

And the foe learns to his cost
That nothing of you has been lost

Do you see, Che, what love can do
For those you loved who now love you?

B. STEPHENS (USA)

Che was the first continental and international Latin American revolutionary that I knew in Cuba. On 1 May, 1964, during a pause in the public holiday, body present and heart faraway, that's how I saw him, solitary in the shade of the statue of Martí, smoking and reading in the smoke some vision, faraway from where or when, travelling through history. I took his photograph and he went on smiling his grave smile, the violent patience of the faraway look in his eyes looking into the future. We were introduced, we had a small coffee, and that was all.

I told my Italian friends in Cuba and afterward my Cuban friends in Italy: 'I could swear that Che is a poet, and I never make a mistake in my intuitions; Che writes poetry. . . .' They laughed in my face. Miguel Barnet answered that his poetry was action, the pistol was his pen. But I was not convinced because Che was a complete man, and he wrote with pen and pistol, with thought as well as action, with words and mind. He was a human message and wrote messages to be read, which must be read with great attention: A complete man with a message that will print itself on the hard face of the earth.

GIANNI TOTI (Italy)

It is three years since I was in Brazil. I saw the misery in the northwest, the peasants grown stupid without even the strength to complain or hate.

Their material conditions have not improved, but for some years since the Cuban Revolution, men like Guevara have been with them. They rouse them and light a fuse of resistance, a revolutionary conscience; they make a decision against all hypocritical reform, disguised as an impossible coexistence with imperialism.

Whoever has been in those hands is conscious that there is no middle of the road. Actions and men seen from Europe can appear irrational, the stuff of historical legend, of courage without end. Yet in South America, these actions and war are the only positive forces, precisely rational for their extreme impetus and total subversion.

In these days, we can say in one breath : Latin America, Cuba, Vietnam – Guevara.

The lesson we learn from him : a total coherence, an extreme force of conscience to fight imperialism, no matter where it may be.

EMILIO VEDOVA (Italy)

He died just when we needed him
More than ever before.
Why did he die?
Was he sick? Had he lost faith?
Was it perhaps a sacrifice?
But if he was sick, why didn't we help him?
He was like a Christ taken down from the Cross ...
I loathe the heroics of pain
I loathe the mystique of resurrection
We abandoned him
When we ought to have helped him with all our might.
The very earth which drank his blood was not his earth;
Only the land where you live is yours.
And now we're turning him into a martyr
To ease our own consciences.
Or am I making a mistake?
Was he perhaps strong and active and full of faith?
Was he perhaps the only one who dared?
Did his death teach us our cowardice?
Learn
Learn
Learn
The struggle continues.

PETER WEISS (Germany)

What can I say to you, Che Guevara?
Only that I feel sorrow
Because I did not know you better.
And shame.
Because I did so little to help.

I am fifty years of age, Che Guevara,
I will not bother to describe myself
I am sure you get the picture.
Even a super-silver stainless blade
Cannot shave away
The grey hostages I have given
To expediency.
The comfortable compromising
And the flatulent phrases.
Such as
'The need to be patient'
And 'to exercise restraint'
The suggestion that Socialism
'Is, perhaps, an old-fashioned notion,
Rendered obsolete by modern technology'
Or that
'Freedom, after all,
Is a relative concept'
Above all,
That 'the hero has no place
In Literature.
Or in Life, for that matter'

You were a real and actual man, Che Guevara
In your dying
There was no myth
No trick to fool the simple.
Your body did not arise on the Third Day.
In practical terms
You are quite dead.

But you have proved to me, Che Guevara
That all the vinegar years
Have not entirely soured the wine of youth.
Freedom,
Is still more than just a word to me.

What do you mean to me, Che Guevara?
Of course, you were a hero.
But I think of you as a friend
As a good comrade
Who is still with us.

Of course, your name will be honoured.
My children and their children
Shall say it as easily
As if it were their own.
But more important than all this
I shall try
A little harder
Because of you
To climb the forbidding and inhospitable mountain.

'Whether he now rests in an anonymous grave, or whether he has, once again, escaped to re-appear elsewhere, this courageous man deserves both respect and honour.' The author of these lines is an American, writing an editorial in the *New York Times*. The man he is describing is, of course, Che Guevara, enemy number one of the United States.

I met him only once, in 1960, in the early days of the Cuban Revolution. He was president of the Bank of Cuba then. On an impulse, I had sent him a telegram from the African capital where I was staying. Two days later, I received an answer : Comandante Ernesto Guevara will see you on Tuesday at noon.

At the appointed time, I was in Havana, in the waiting room of the Bank of Cuba. Two or three minutes later, the door of the lift opened and a very young, square-shouldered man with an extremely pale face strode into the room. As he came over to shake hands with me, I neither noticed his straggly beard nor his blue-black beret with its red star. I saw only his large black eyes which smiled when his lips smiled. I had expected to meet a hard man, and instead there stood before me an almost timid man in whom gentleness was the key-note.

We spoke for three and a half hours and our conversation made a profound impact on me. Guevara was not like any of the other outstanding men I have met before or since. A lot has been said about his romanticism, his poetry; a lot has also been said about his revolutionary intransigeance. Yet he was too precise, too organised, to be a poet or a romantic; and the man who wrote, 'I must say, even at the risk of seeming ridiculous, that the true revolutionary is guided by motives of love,' cannot be that professional advocate of violent revolution that some have made him out to be.

The man who, at the age of twenty-four, abandons his country, his studies, his family and his middle-class standard of living to set off on a bicycle towards the unknown; the man who, at that age, has already gone beyond the narrow confines of patriotism to join the

As Minister, Che Guevara
inspects grain production.

struggle against injustice in Guatemala, then Mexico, then Cuba; the man who, twelve years later, with the final outcome of the revolution he helped bring about still in balance, leaves it in the hands of his companions-in-arms and sets off again, writing to Fidel: 'Other nations in the world call for my modest efforts. . . . That if my final hour comes beneath other skies, my last thought will be for this people and especially for you. . . . That I leave my wife and my children nothing, and I am not sorry, but glad it should be so. That I can do nothing for them as the State will give them enough to live on and will educate them . . .' that man has no equal in the world today. He reconciles the most pessimistic to the human race. I feel proud that he was a citizen of the Third World.

Like all great men, he knew he was different from the others, more sensitive, more complete. What distinguished him from the other great men and that he had common with Lenin, was that it never was a source of vanity for him and that he never felt the least contempt for others. On the contrary, he would have wanted all men to feel as he did; at most, he sometimes felt irritated or distressed that they did not. The one idea which obsessed him all his life was : to transform the alienated man of today into the new liberated man of tomorrow. 'Each individual would feel inwardly richer and more responsible within himself. The vital thing is for men to become more conscious each day of the need to incorporate themselves within their society and at the same time to realise their own significance within that society.'

'The road is long and some of it is unmapped. We will often have to turn back, and at times we will find that we have gone too fast and left the masses behind. At other times, because we will have gone too slowly, we will feel the masses pressing at our heels. As revolutionaries, we try to go as quickly as possible, clearing the way, but we know that we have to rely on the masses and that they will advance rapidly only if they have our example to follow.'

The man who wrote these lines, who did what Guevara has done, and who lived his life, deserves the respect of everyone, including those to whom his name was anathema.

If he is dead, as we are told he is, he died fighting in the service of the idea which never left him, with the certainty that he had 'worked to consolidate the revolution honourably and with enough devotion.' Let us only hope that, in the last instants of his life, he kept all his faith.

BECHIR BEN YAHMED (Tunisia)

How Che Died

It was one of Che's habits during his guerrilla life to jot down meticulously the day's events in a personal diary. On long marches across rough and difficult terrain or through damp forests, when the lines of men, always weighed down with rucksacks and weapons and ammunition, stopped to rest for a moment, or when the column received orders to halt and pitch camp at the end of an exhausting day, Che (as he was affectionately called by the Cubans from the start) would be seen taking out his notebook and setting down impressions in his tiny, almost illegible doctor's handwriting. He later made use of the notes he managed to preserve, to write his magnificent historical reminiscences of the Cuban Revolutionary War, so full of value from a revolutionary, educational and human point of view.

Once again, thanks to Che's enduring habit of noting the principal events of each day, we have access to priceless information, detailed and rigorously exact, about those last heroic months of his life in Bolivia.

He constantly used these notes, which were not really intended for publication, as a tool with which to evaluate events, men and the general situation. They also provided an outlet for his acutely observant and analytical spirit, which was often tinged with a keen sense of humour. He kept up the habit so conscientiously that the notes remain coherent from beginning to end.

It must be remembered that this diary was written during extremely rare moments of rest from superhuman and back-breaking physical effort, without mentioning Che's exhausting responsibilities as a guerrilla leader during the difficult early days of this form of struggle, which unfolded in particularly hard material circumstances; this goes to show once again the kind of man Che was, and his strength of will.

There are detailed analyses of each day's incidents in this diary, exposing the errors, criticisms and recriminations, which are an inevitable part of any revolutionary guerrilla.

Criticisms of this sort have to be made incessantly in a guerrilla detachment, especially during the first stage, when there is only a small nucleus of men who are permanently exposed to extremely

adverse material conditions and an enemy which is far superior in number; at such times, the least oversight, the most significant error of judgement, can be fatal, and the chief has to be very exacting. He must turn each event or minor incident, however trivial, into a lesson for fighters and future leaders of new guerrilla detachments.

The training of a guerrilla force makes constant demands on the honour and conscience of each man. Che knew how to touch the most sensitive cords in a revolutionary's heart. When he told Marcos, after repeated warnings, that he might have to give him a dishonourable discharge, Marcos replied, 'I'd rather you shot me!' Later on, Marcos bravely gave up his life. All the men in whom Che placed his trust and yet had to admonish for one reason or another in the course of the struggle, felt the same way as Marcos. Che was a humane and comradely leader who also knew when to be demanding, even severe at times. But he was always far harder on himself than on others and he based his discipline on the moral conscience of the guerrillas and on the tremendous force of his personal example.

Yankee aggression may use our solidarity with the revolutionary movement as a pretext to attack us, but this will never be the true cause. To deny solidarity in order to eliminate the pretext would be an absurd, ostrich-like policy totally alien to the international nature of today's social revolutions. To disown our solidarity with the revolutionary movement would not just mean denying the pretext, but would actually be tantamount to supporting Yankee imperialism and its policy of world enslavement and domination.

Cuba is a small and economically underdeveloped country, like all countries which have been dominated and exploited by colonialism and imperialism for centuries. It is only 90 miles away from the coast of the United States, and has a Yankee naval base on its territory. There are many economic and social obstacles to its development. Our country has known periods of great danger since our victorious Revolution, but that will not make us yield or weaken; a consistent line of revolutionary conduct is impervious to hardships.

Imperialism also has personal reasons of its own: Che and his extraordinary example are constantly growing in strength throughout the world. His ideas, his portrait and his name are banners in the struggle against injustice by the oppressed and the exploited and they arouse passionate enthusiasm in the students and intellectuals everywhere.

Even in the United States, the black movement and the ever-increasing number of radical students have adopted Che's image. His photographs are paraded as emblems of the struggle in the most militant civil rights marches and demonstrations against the aggression in Vietnam. Rarely, if ever, in history has one man's image, name and example spread so rapidly and so completely. The reason is

Opposite: Che Guevara with Fidel Castro.

Che Guevara in Bolivia before his death in October, 1967.

that Che stood for the spirit of internationalism in its purest and most disinterested form, and it is this spirit which characterizes the world of today and, even more so, the world of tomorrow.

This amazing figure who symbolizes world-wide revolutionary struggle even in the capitals of the imperialist and colonial world came from a continent which was once oppressed by colonial powers and which is now exploited and kept in the most criminal state of underdevelopment by Yankee imperialism.

The Yankee imperialists are frightened of Che's potent example and of everything that helps to spread his reputation. This is the greatest value of the diary : it is the living expression of an extraordinary personality, a lesson for guerrilla fighters written in the heat and suspense of each day. That is what makes it explosive; it is the proof that men in Latin America are not helpless against those who try to enslave them with mercenary armies.

It could well be that many so-called revolutionaries, opportunists and impostors of every sort, who call themselves Marxists, Communists and a variety of other names, would also prefer the diary to remain unknown. They do not hesitate to dismiss Che as a deluded adventurer, or at best an idealist, claiming that his death was the swansong of revolutionary armed struggle in Latin America. 'If Che, the greatest exponent of such ideas and an experienced guerrilla fighter was killed in a guerrilla war and if his movement did not liberate Bolivia, that proves he was completely wrong!' That is the way they argue; and how many of those miserable characters rejoiced at the news of Che's death, not even ashamed that their position and their reasoning coincided perfectly with those of the most reactionary oligarchies and with imperialism!

They reasoned like this to justify themselves or to justify treacherous leaders who did not hesitate occasionally to pretend to endorse armed struggle while in fact – as has been discovered since – their true purpose was to destroy guerrilla movements in the bud, to slow down all revolutionary action, and to put in its place their own absurd and despicable political deals, being utterly incapable of taking any other line of conduct. They also needed to justify those who lacked the will to fight and who will never fight for the liberation of their people, but who have turned revolutionary ideology into a caricature of itself, until it is nothing more than a dogma and an opiate without any genuine meaning or message for the masses. Such men have converted the organizations for the struggle of the masses into instruments of conciliation with both foreign and domestic exploiters and advocates of policies that go against the interests of the exploited Latin-American people.

Che envisaged death as a natural and probable part of the process, and he tried, especially in his last documents, to underline the fact that this eventuality could not slow down the inevitable march of Revolution in Latin America. He emphasized this in his message to the Tricontinental Congress: 'Our every action is a battle cry against imperialism . . . wherever death may surprise us, let it be welcome so long as our battle cry may have reached some receptive ear and another hand may reach out to pick up our weapons.'

Che looked upon himself as a soldier of the revolution and never worried about surviving it. Those who imagine that Che's ideas failed because of the outcome of the struggle in Bolivia might as well use this simplistic argument to say that many of the great revolutionary precursors and revolutionary thinkers, including the founders of Marxism, were also failures because they were unable to see the culmination of their life's work and died before their noble efforts were crowned with success.

In Cuba, the ultimate triumph of a process which was set into motion 100 years ago was not halted by the deaths of Martí and Maceo in combat, followed by the Yankee intervention at the end of the War of Independence which frustrated the immediate objective of their struggle, nor was it halted by the assassination of a brilliant theoretician of socialist revolution like Julio Antonio Mella, murdered by agents in the service of imperialism. And absolutely no one can doubt the rightness of these great men's cause and the line of conduct, or the validity of their basic ideas which have always served as an inspiration to Cuban revolutionaries.

We can see from Che's diary how genuine was the possibility of success and what an extraordinary catalyst the guerrilla proved to be. On one occasion, observing obvious symptoms of weakness and rapid decline in the Bolivian régime, he noted: 'The government is disintegrating rapidly; what a pity we do not have 100 more men right now.'

Che knew from his Cuban experience how many times our small guerrilla detachment was on the point of being exterminated. It could have happened because, in war, one depends so much on chance and circumstances. And if it had happened, would it have given anybody the right to say that our line of conduct had been wrong, using our example to discourage revolution and inculcate people with a sense of helplessness? The revolutionary process has known setbacks many times in history. Did we not, in Cuba, experience Moncada only six years before the final triumph of our people's armed struggle?

Between the attack of 26 July, 1953, on the Moncada Fortress and the *Granma* landing on 2 December, 1956, there were many who believed that the revolutionary struggle in Cuba was hopeless, that a handful of fighters would not stand a chance against a modern and well-equipped army, and that those fighters could only be looked upon as idealists and dreamers 'who were utterly wrong.' The terrible defeat and the total dispersal of the inexperienced guerrilla detachment on 5 December, 1956, seemed to prove the pessimists' point of view completely. . . . But, only twenty-five months later, the remnants of that guerrilla force had acquired enough strength and experience to rout the army totally.

There will be good excuses not to fight at all times and in every circumstance, and that will be the surest way never to win freedom. Che did not outlive his ideas, but he gave them added strength by shedding his blood for them. His pseudo-revolutionary critics, with their political cowardice and their permanent lack of action, will quite certainly live to see the day when their stupidity will be exposed.

It will be noticed in this diary that one of these revolutionary specimens becoming more and more common in Latin America, Mario Monje, brandishing his title of Secretary of the Communist Party of Bolivia, disputed with Che the political and military leadership of the movement. He went on to say that, for this, he would resign his party position, and seemed to think that it was quite enough to have once held such a title to claim the prerogative.

Needless to say, Mario Monje had no guerrilla experience and had never fought a combat in his life; without mentioning the fact that his personal notion of Communism should have rid him of such narrow and vulgar chauvinism long before then, just as our ancestors got rid of it to fight the first round for Independence.

If this is their concept of what the anti-imperialist struggle on this

Opposite: Che Guevara in a jungle hide-out in Bolivia.

continent should be, then these so-called 'Communist leaders' have not progressed further in the notion of internationalism than the Indian tribes which were conquered by the colonisers.

And so, this Communist Party boss proceeded to make ridiculous, shameful and undeserved claims for leadership in a country called Bolivia, with a historic capital called Sucre, both named in honour of the first liberators who came from Venezuela; and Bolivia owed its final liberation to the political, military and organizational talent of an authentic revolutionary genius who did not limit his beliefs to the narrow, artificial and even unjust frontiers of that country.

Bolivia does not have an outlet to the sea; if it were liberated, it would need the revolutionary victory of its neighbours more than any other country so as not to be subjected to the most intolerable blockade. And Che was the man who could have accelerated the process with his tremendous prestige, abilities and experience.

Che had established relations with Bolivian Communist leaders and militants before the split that occurred within the Party, calling on them to help the revolutionary movement in South America. Some of those militants, with the party's permission, collaborated with him on various tasks for years. The party split created a new situation in which the militants who had worked with Che found themselves in different camps. But Che did not look upon the struggle in Bolivia as an isolated cause; he saw it as part of a revolutionary movement for liberation which would soon extend to other countries of South America. His aim was to organize a movement that would be free of sectarianism and that could be joined by all those who wanted to fight for the liberation of Bolivia and other Latin American countries subjected to imperialism. During the initial phase of preparation for a guerrilla base, however, Che had relied chiefly on the aid of a courageous and discreet group which remained in Monje's party after the split. It was out of deference to them that he first invited Monje to visit the camp, although he felt no sympathy for him whatsoever. Later, Che also invited Moisés Guevara, the political leader of the miners who had left Monje's party to help create another organization, from which he finally had to withdraw as well because he disagreed with Oscar Zamora. Zamora, another Monje, had agreed to work with Che in organizing armed guerrilla warfare in Bolivia, but he later withdrew his support and sat back like a coward when the hour for action had struck. In the name of 'Marxist-Leninism,' Zamora became one of Che's most vicious critics after his death, while Moisés Guevara unhesitatingly joined Che, as he had agreed to do long before Che came to Bolivia, offering his support and heroically giving up his life to the revolutionary cause.

The group of Bolivian guerrilla fighters, who had remained loyal to Monje's organization until then, did the same. Directed by Inti and

Opposite: Che Guevara drinks maté during a guerrilla campaign.

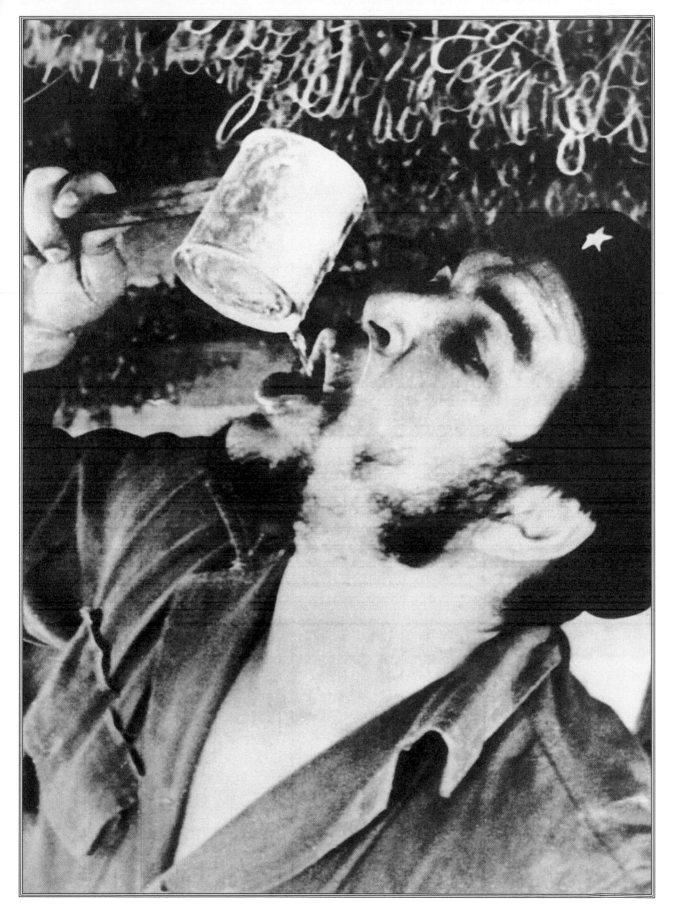

Coco Peredo, who later proved their courage and their worth as combatants, they broke away from Monje and became staunch supporters of Che. But Monje was not pleased with the outcome and began to sabotage the movement, dissuading militant and well-trained Communists from going to join the guerrilla. Actions of this nature show how incompetent leaders who are imposters and manipulators can criminally check the development within the revolutionary framework of men who are completely ready and able to fight.

Che was a man who never took any personal interest in rank, position or honours, but he was absolutely convinced of one thing: that in revolutionary guerrilla warfare, which is the basic form of action needed to liberate the peoples of Latin America given the economic, political and social condition of almost all those countries, the military and political leadership of the guerrilla has to be unified and the struggle can only be led from within the guerrilla and not from comfortable bureaucratic offices in the cities. He was determined not to give in on this point or to hand over to an inexperienced blockhead with narrow, chauvinistic views, the leadership of a guerrilla nucleus, which was ultimately destined to spread the struggle across all of South America. Che felt that chauvinism, which so often contaminates even the revolutionary elements in various Latin American countries, was something to be fought against, an absurdly reactionary and sterile attitude. As he said in his message to the Tricontinental : 'And let us develop a true proletarian internationalism . . . the flag under which we fight would be the sacred cause of redeeming humanity. To die under the flag of Vietnam, of Venezuela, of Guatemala, of Laos, of Guinea, of Colombia, of Bolivia, of Brazil – to name only a few scenes of today's armed struggle – would be equally glorious and desirable for an American, an Asian, an African, even a European. Each drop of blood spilt by a man in any country under whose flag he was not born is an experience passed on to those who survive, to be added later to the liberation struggle of his country. And each nation liberated is a phase won in the battle for the liberation of one's own country.'

Che also believed that fighters from different Latin American countries should participate in the development of the guerrilla and that Bolivia's guerrilla force ought to act as a school for revolutionaries who would learn in combat. To help him in this task he needed, along with the Bolivians, a small nucleus of experienced guerrillas, nearly all of them his comrades in the Sierra Maestra at the time of Cuba's revolutionary war; he knew the aptitudes, courage and spirit of sacrifice of these men, and not one of them failed him in his demands, abandoned him or surrendered.

Throughout the Bolivian campaign, Che displayed those exemplary qualities of endurance, ability and stoicism, for which he was so rightly famous. It can truly be said that, knowing the importance of the task he had set out to accomplish, he proceeded to go about it with the most faultless sense of responsibility at all times. On every occasion that the guerrilla acted carelessly, he quickly took the fact into account, corrected it, and set it down in his diary.

The most incredible succession of adverse factors combined against Che, such as the loss of contact with a group of his fighters containing several valuable men, some of them ill, others convalescing. The separation, which was only intended to last for a few days, was drawn out interminably for months, during which Che made every effort to find them over extremely difficult terrain. During this period, his asthma became a serious problem; normally, a simple medicine would have kept it under control easily, but without that medicine, it became a terrible enemy which attacked him mercilessly. This occurred because the stores of medicine wisely stocked by the guerrilla were discovered and seized by the enemy. The evolution of the struggle was gravely affected by this event as well as by the liquidation, at the end of August, of the group with which Che had lost contact. Yet Che managed to overcome his physical deterioration with a will of steel, and he never allowed it to affect his morale or to stand in the way of action.

Che repeatedly came into contact with the Bolivian peasants and he could not have been surprised by their extremely wary and distrustful nature, as he had had dealings with them on other occasions and knew their mentality well. He realized that it would be a long, difficult and patient job to win them over to his cause, but he never doubted for a moment that he would succeed in the end.

If we examine the sequence of events carefully, we will see that even in September, a few weeks before Che's death, when the number of men on whom he could rely had dwindled drastically, the guerrilla still maintained its capacity for development and some of the Bolivian cadres, such as the brothers Inti and Coco Peredo, were beginning to show terrific potential as leaders. But the Higueras ambush, the only successful army action against Che's detachment, proved to be an irreversible setback for the guerrilla. This action killed off the advance party and wounded several men as they were moving in broad daylight to another zone where the peasants were more developed politically. This objective is not mentioned in the diary, but survivors have testified that it was their goal. Of course, it was dangerous to advance by day along a road they had been following for several days, inevitably coming into contact with local people, in an area which was new to them. And it must have seemed obvious that the army would try to stop them somewhere along the way. But Che, fully conscious of the risk he was running, decided to try his luck so as to help the Doctor who was in very bad physical shape.

The day before the ambush, Che wrote: 'We reached Pujio but there were people there who had seen us the day before, which means that news of us has spread by word of mouth . . . It is becoming dangerous to march with the mules, but I want the Doctor to travel as comfortably as possible as he is very weak.'

The following day, he wrote: 'At 13:00, the advance party left to try and reach Jagüey and to make a decision there about the mules and the Doctor.' In other words, Che was trying to find a solution concerning the sick man in order to abandon their route and take necessary precautions. But that same afternoon, before reaching Jagüey, the advance party fell into the fatal ambush from which the detachment never recovered.

A few days later, encircled in the Yuro ravine, Che fought his last combat.

What this handful of revolutionaries accomplished remains extremely impressive. Even their struggle against the hostile environment they had selected is an unforgettable saga of heroism. Never before in history had such a small number of men set out on such a gigantic undertaking. Their faith, their absolute conviction that the great revolutionary process could be triggered off in Latin America, their confidence and determination as they went to accomplish this objective, give us some idea of their stature.

Once Che said to the guerrilla fighters of Bolivia: 'This form of struggle gives us the opportunity to turn ourselves into revolutionaries, the highest state a man can reach; but it also allows us to graduate as men; those who cannot reach either of these two states must say so and give up the struggle.'

The men who fought with him until the end proved they deserved both of these titles. They symbolize the kind of revolutionaries and men which history needs right now for a really difficult and arduous mission : the revolutionary transformation of Latin America.

During the first fight for independence, the enemy our ancestors fought was a decadent colonial power. The enemy which today's revolutionaries have to reckon with is the most powerful bastion of the imperialist camp, the most highly advanced, technically and industrially. It was this enemy which re-organized and re-equipped the army of Bolivia after the people had crushed the previous repressive military forces. It was this enemy which immediately sent weapons and military advisers to fight against the guerrilla, just as it always has given military and technical aid to every force of repression on this continent. And if that does not suffice, this enemy intervenes directly and sends in troops, as happened in Santo Domingo.

You need the kind of revolutionaries and men that Che described to fight against such an enemy. Without such revolutionaries and men, ready to do what they did, without their spiritual strength to tackle the vast obstacles in their way, without their permanent readiness to die at any moment, without their profound belief in the justness of their cause, without their utter faith in the invincible strength of the people, faced with the might of Yankee imperialism as it throws its military, technical and economic weight around in every corner of the world, the liberation of the peoples of this continent will never be accomplished.

The people themselves in North America are beginning to realize that the monstrous political superstructure which governs their country has for quite a time been totally different from the idyllic bourgeois republic which its founders established nearly two hundred years ago. Their distress grows as they watch the moral barbarism of an irrational, alienating, dehumanized and brutal system which is making an ever-increasing number of victims among the citizens of the U.S., through aggressive wars, political crimes and racial folly; they see human beings turned into mere cogs of a machine; they see the disgusting way in which economic, scientific and human resources are squandered on a vast, reactionary and repressive military apparatus when three-quarters of the world is underdeveloped and hungry.

But only the revolutionary transformation of Latin America would enable the people of the United States to settle their private score with imperialism, while at the same time the growing revolt within the U.S. itself against imperialist policy could become a decisive factor in the revolutionary struggle of Latin America.

And if this half of the American continent does not undergo a profound revolutionary transformation, the fantastic inequality which presently exists between the two halves of the continent will continue to increase. This imbalance began at the turn of the century, when the U.S. rapidly industrialized, and at the same rate, acquired imperial aspirations as it followed the dynamic course of its own social and economic evolution. Meanwhile, the other Balkanized nations of the American continent remained weak and stagnant, submissively yielding to the yoke of feudal oligarchies and their reactionary armies. In another twenty years, this terrible inequality will have increased a hundredfold, not just economically, scientifically and technically, but above all politically.

If this goes on, we will become progressively poorer, weaker, more dependent on, and enslaved by imperialism. This sombre prospect looms over all the underdeveloped nations of Africa and Asia as well.

If the industrialized and educated nations of Europe, with their Common Market and their pooled scientific institutes, are worrying about getting left behind and are afraid of becoming the economic colonies of Yankee imperialism, what does the future have in store for the people of Latin America?

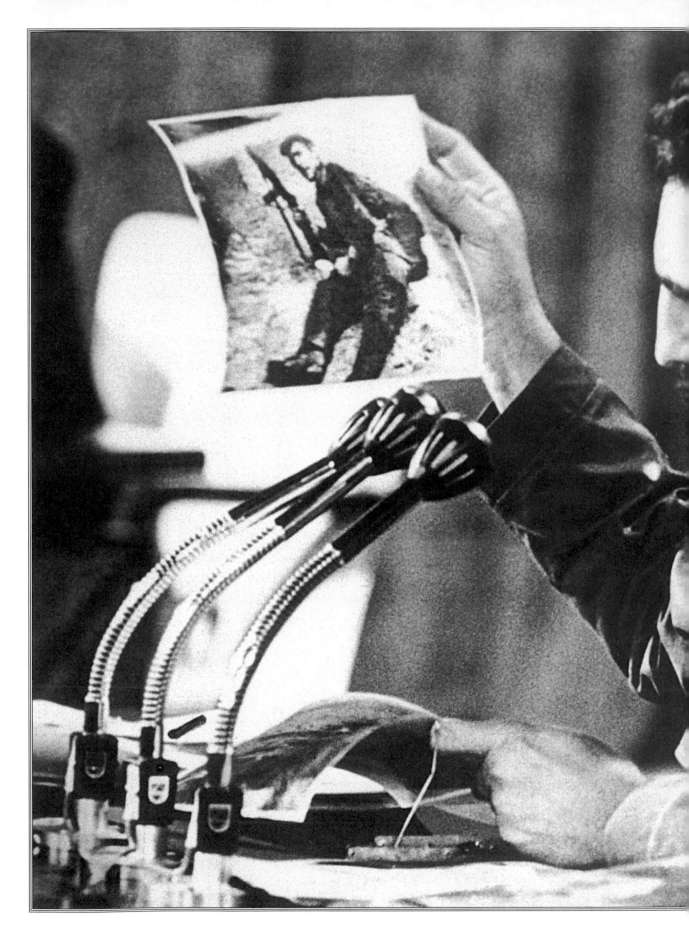

Fidel Castro announcing to the people of Cuba on 10 October, 1967, that the picture of murdered Che Guevara in Bolivia is authentic.

Perhaps some liberal or bourgeois reformist or pseudo-revolutionary impostor, incapable of action, has found a solution to this genuine and incontestable situation which decisively affects the destiny of our people; if so, let him speak up. Let him tell us what he proposes in place of a profound and urgent revolutionary transformation, one which would polarize all the moral, material and human resources needed in this part of the world to make up for the economic, scientific and technical backwardness of centuries, even greater when we compare it to the industrialized world which makes us and will go on making us its serfs, especially the United States. If he can produce the magic formula which will accomplish this in a different way, which will wipe out the oligarchies, the despots, the petty politicians, all the lackeys of the Yankee monopolies, their masters, and if his solution can be applied as rapidly as circumstances require, then let him raise his hand and challenge Che.

But no one has proposed an honest alternative or a consequent line of conduct which would give genuine hope to the 300 million human beings, most of them desperately poor, who make up the population of Latin America; not forgetting that those 300 million will have become 600 million within the next 25 years, all of whom have a right to a decent living, a culture and civilization. It would therefore be more decorous to fall silent before the gesture made by Che and by those who fell at his side, courageously defending his ideas. Because of what that handful of men did, their noble ideal, which was to redeem a continent, will remain the highest proof of what will-power, heroism and human greatness can do. It is their example, which will awaken the conscience of the Latin American people in the struggle to come; Che's heroic call will reach the receptive ears of the poor and the exploited for whom he gave his life. And many hands will stretch out to pick up weapons and to conquer freedom once and for all.

Che wrote his last lines on 7 October. On the following day, at 13:00 hours, in a narrow ravine where they had decided to wait until nightfall to break out of the encirclement, a large enemy troop made contact with them. Although reduced in number, the group of men who now made up the detachment fought heroically until dusk, from individual positions on the floor of the ravine and on ledges higher up, against the mass of soldiers who had surrounded and attacked them. There were no survivors among those who were fighting close to Che. Near him were the Doctor, whose very bad state of health he had noted earlier, and a Peruvian fighter also in extremely poor physical condition; it therefore seems most likely that Che was doing everything in his power to protect the retreat of these two comrades to a safer place, until he himself was wounded. The Doctor was not killed during this fight, but several days later, quite near the Yuro ravine. The guerrillas had great difficulty locating each other visually, because the terrain was so irregular and rocky. At times, they could not see one another at all. Some of the men, including Inti Peredo, who were defending the other entrance of the ravine several hundred metres from Che, held off the attack until dark and were then able to slip away from the enemy, heading for the spot where they had pre-arranged to meet.

It has been established that Che, although wounded, continued to fight until the barrel of his M-2 was destroyed by a bullet, making it totally useless. The pistol he was carrying did not have a magazine. It was only due to these incredible circumstances that they were able to catch him alive. The wounds in his legs, although not fatal, made it impossible for him to walk unaided.

He was taken to the village of Higueras and remained alive for another 24 hours, more or less. He refused to say a single word to his captors and slapped a drunken officer who tried to taunt him.

Barrientos, Ovanda and other top military chiefs met in La Paz and decided, in cold blood, to assassinate Che. The way they proceeded to carry out this underhand agreement in the school of Higueras is now known. Major Miguel Ayoroa and Colonel Andrés Selnich, two Rangers trained by the Yankees, ordered a non-commissioned officer, Mario Terán, to murder Che. Terán went in, completely drunk, and Che, who had heard the shots which had just killed a Bolivian and a Peruvian fighter, seeing the brute hesitate, said to him firmly, 'Shoot. Don't be afraid.' Terán left the room and his superiors, Ayoroa and Selnich, had to repeat the order which he finally carried out, firing his machine-gun at Che from the waist down. The official tale that Che had died a few hours after the combat was already in circulation; this was why his executioners gave orders not to shoot him in the chest or the head, so as not to produce instantly fatal wounds. Che's agony was thus cruelly prolonged until a sergeant, who was also drunk, finally killed him with a pistol shot to the left side. The whole procedure was in brutal contrast with the respect Che never once failed to show for the lives of the many Bolivian officers and soldiers he had taken prisoner.

Those last hours of his life, spent in the hands of his despicable enemies, must have been bitter for him; but no man was better prepared than Che to face an ordeal of this kind.

Hasta la Victoria Siempre!

FIDEL CASTRO

Régis Debray

The Author of REVOLUTION WITHIN THE REVOLUTION?, the Frenchman Régis Debray, gave this evidence at his trial on the charge of meeting with Che Guevara and his group during the Bolivian Campaign.

These are not guerrillas, the prosecuting attorney stated later, because they do not fight under any flag. They have made no declaration of war. It is quite possible that, since they were taken by surprise by a sudden army attack, the guerrillas did not have time to send a declaration to the outside world, in the form of leaflets or communiqués, for example. It is possible that this was a mistake. At least that is my personal opinion. But this does not concern the court. The important thing is that the guerrillas did have a flag, the highest and noblest in all Latin America, and that flag is the name of Che. The army knew this before going into action, and everything possible was done to hide the fact, to hold back, for example, guerrilla communiqués and Army of National Liberation war dispatches. Yet they later seemed surprised because the flag had not appeared. But, above all, the prosecuting attorney states, they cannot be compared with the guerrilla fighters for independence because they are foreigners.

It is true there were foreigners among them, but naturally a minority. The vast majority were Bolivians, but there were Peruvians, Cubans and one Argentinian. Is this by any chance something new in the history of Bolivia? Is this by any chance in contradiction with the profoundly national and patriotic nature of this liberation struggle? We need not cite the examples here of Bolívar, Sucre, Santa Cruz, Belgrano and the four reinforcement armies from Argentina; of the Venezuelans, Chileans and Argentinians who founded Bolivia and all of Latin America. We are only speaking of guerrillas who fought for independence – and not the top leaders of the regular armies. We are speaking of the Padillas, the Warnes, the Lanzas. I have here in front of me a book published by the San Francisco Xavier University of Sucre, the Diary of a Soldier of Alto Perú Independence, written about 1820 by a guerrilla who fought in the Sicasica and Ayopaya valleys, at the time of Bolivia's birth as a nation. He was, as a matter of fact, one of the 'factions' – that is, of the guerrillas commanded by José Manuel Lanza. And the following is taken from the prologue: 'Most members of the faction are from the valleys – that is, they are Indians or mestizos. But the faction also includes a host of unseasoned armed men from many places and of all kinds, unusual groups grafted onto the main stem. Of course in the Alto Perú faction there are many from other parts of the country: Orureños, Cochabambinos, Paceños, and even Cruceños ... There are also soldiers from other parts of the Americas in the faction: some Bonaerenses (inhabitants of Buenos Aires), Tucumanos and Paraguayans, left-overs from Rondeau's Argentine expedition. Others present in the faction include Peruvians from Cuzco, and there are also blacks. And even Englishmen – who arrived in the valley God knows how or when – are included in the Indian-mestizo force fighting against Spain in the southernmost part of the Alto Perú mountain area.'

It is not the job of a Frenchman to teach a Bolivian military prosecuting attorney the history of his country. But since so much reference has been made to that history, gentleman, here are the facts of history. Thus, Bolivia was liberated from the Spanish by men who came from every corner of Latin America to help found Bolivia and all of Latin America. And similarly the same fraternal union of Latin Americans, tested in combat and the life of the battle campaign itself, will liberate Bolivia from Yankee imperialism. A socialist Bolivia will be founded, and the whole continent, whose centre is Bolivia, will do the same.

For Che the true difference, the true frontier, is not the one which separates a Bolivian from a Peruvian, a Peruvian from an Argentinian, an Argentinian from a Cuban. It is the one which separates Latin Americans from Yankees. That is why Bolivians, Peruvians, Cubans and Argentinians are all brothers in the struggle,

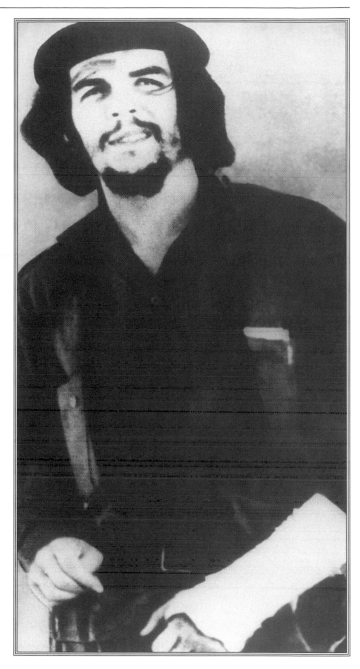

Che Guevara, after being wounded in action.

and where one nationality is fighting, the others should also be fighting, because they have everything in common, the same history, the same language, the same patriots, the same destiny, and even the same master, the same exploiter, the same enemy which treats them all alike: Yankee imperialism. 'In South American,' said Bolívar, 'the fight is for every man, no matter where he may be.' When in 1821 Bolívar offered Pueyrredón, Chief Director of the Río de la Plata Provinces, brotherhood and the direct aid of Venezuelans, he sent the following message: 'All the republics fighting against Spain are united by one implicit and actual accord, by the identical nature of our cause, principles and interests; thus it seems our action should be the same, united action.'

This implicit accord became a flesh and blood reality in the army that went to liberate Bajo and Alto Perú, to create Bolivia, that army which the Liberator reviewed shortly before Junin, in Pasco, 'where there were gathered together men from Caracas, Panama, Quito, Lima, Chile and Buenos Aires: men who had fought at Maipú in Chile, at San Lorenzo on the coast of Panama, at Carabobo in Venezuela and at Pichincha at the foot of the Chimborazo.' Che, Bolívar's historical heir, did not have time to amass that army in the jungles of south-east Bolivia, but that was the idea. It is difficult, it seems utopian, but it is invincible, and will win. In his letter of 1815 from Jamaica, Bolívar launched the idea of an integrated Latin America, far removed from criminal individualisms, and the idea of integral Americans was born as well. A century and a half ago, this was a premature vision. And today it still seems premature to some, and that is why Che died; but his death was not in vain. Che will not have 'sowed in shifting sands.' He took up the tradition of liberation, the most patriotic, the most Bolivian, the most Latin American of traditions.

Others have taken up chauvinism in the spirit of individualist rancour, which has no roots in any part at all of the history of independence. When a tiger is marauding in a neighbourhood, and a lamb, just one of the flock, wants to keep its neighbour away by saying, 'You are not from here, this part of the pasture does not belong to you, you have to stay in your country, which is on the other side of the river,' this lamb, instead of getting all the others to unite against their principal enemy, betrays those of his own class, places their lives in danger as well as his own. He certainly must have made a deal to ally himself with the tiger, but he is wrong if he thinks that he can so escape the tiger's claws. No treaty of alliance can be valid between a carnivorous nation and one that can be eaten up, such a choice morsel as Bolivia. Chauvinism, reactionary nationalism, is nothing more than a sentimental façade for the cold bricks of a sell-out treaty.

I am about to conclude. A lawyer for the civil party expressed his fear that the defence, by asking for clemency, might deny the winners

The Cry of the Survivor

Guerrilla warfare in Bolivia is not dead!

It has just begun.

The Bolivian guerrillas are now fully on their way, and we will unflaggingly carry the struggle through to the brilliant victory of the revolutionary forces that will bring socialism to Latin America.

Our country has lived through – in principle – a revolutionary experience of undreamt continental proportions. The beginning of our struggle was accompanied by tragic adversity. The irreparable physical death of our friend and comrade, our Major Ernest Che Guevara, as well as of many other fighters, has been a rude blow to us. They, who were the purest and noblest of our continent's generation, did not hesitate to offer up the only thing they could – their lives – on the altar of human redemption.

But these painful events, far from frightening us, strengthen our revolutionary awareness; increase our determination to fight for a just cause; make it stauncher; and forge, in the purifying and bloody crucible of war, new fighters and leaders, who will honour and pay homage to those who have already fallen.

We know what we are fighting for. We are not waging war for the sake of war. We are not wishful thinkers. We are not fighting for the sake of personal or party ambition. We have confidence in man as a human being.

Our single and final goal is the liberation of Latin America, which is more than our continent; it is rather our homeland, temporarily torn into twenty republics.

We are convinced that the dream of Bolívar and Che – that of ting Latin America both politically and geographically – will be attained through armed struggle, which is the only dignified, honest, glorious, and irreversible method which will motivate the people. No other form of struggle is purer. Guerrilla warfare is the most effective and correct method of armed struggle.

For this reason, as long as there is a single honest man in Latin America, guerrilla warfare will not die. Armed struggle will surge ahead vigorously, until all of the people awake and rise up in arms against the common enemy, American imperialism.

Guerrilla warfare in Bolivia is not dead; it has just begun.

We have lost a battle in which the maximum leader of the oppressed people, Major Ernesto Che Guevara, gave his life.

But our war continues, and we will never stop, because we who fought at Che's side do not recognise the word 'surrender'. His blood and that of other fighters, spilled on the soil of Bolivia, will give life to the seed of liberation and will turn our continent into a volcano, spewing forth fire and destruction on imperialism.

We will be the triumphant Vietnam that Che, the romantic and heroic visionary, dreamed of and loved.

We are determined to win or die for these ideals.

Cuban comrades died for these ideals.

Peruvian comrades died for these ideals.

Argentinian comrades died for these ideals.

Bolivian comrades died for these ideals.

Honour and glory for Tania, Joaquín, Juan Pablo Chang, Moisés Guevara, Jorge Vázquez, Aniceto Reynaga, Antonio Jiménez, and Coco Peredo; honour and glory for each and every one of those who died with weapons in hand, because they understood that, as Che said:

'Wherever death may surprise us, let it be welcome, so long as our battle cry reach some receptive ear and another hand reach out to pick up our weapons, and other men come forward to intone our funeral dirge with the staccato of machine-guns and new cries of battle and victory.'

Our banners bear crêpe, but they will never be lowered.

The National Liberation Army considers itself the heir to the teachings and example of Che, the new Bolívar of Latin America.

Those who cravenly murdered him will never kill his thought and his example.

Let the imperialists and their lackeys withhold their songs of victory, because the war has not ended; it has just begun.

We will return to the mountains!

Bolivia will again resound to our cry of
VICTORY OR DEATH!

Bolivia, July, 1968

INTI PEREDO

The Death and Life of Che Guevara

The care that the Bolivian army authorities took to assassinate the wounded Che and to burn his body and scatter his ashes showed the fear that the military governments of Latin America felt about Che's legend and his dream of uniting the continent through armed struggle. They knew that his cause would not die with his body. They might make cinders of his corpse, but they could not make ashes of his ideal. Pombo, who had been Che's bodyguard and who escaped from Bolivia back to Cuba, refused to admit the failure of the Bolivian attempt. "It didn't fail," he said. "We lost a battle." And he continued, "The guerrilla group, like men, is at birth an almost defenceless creature, a child. If ours had survived, he would have grown and developed. But in Bolivia there was one failure: they discovered us too early and we had to fight." The idea of an armed continental revolution spreading from a guerrilla focus near the centre of the continent was not dead among the followers of Che. It was postponed until the next rising.

In death, Che had more influence than when he was alive. Dead men may tell no tales, but they can make a legend. Che was not only one of the more heroic men of his age; he was also one of the more intelligent, more original, more ascetic, more radical, more human, and most beautiful men of the future. His face launched a thousand turmoils, his words a hundred revolts. He provided the Marxists with their first saint, who dedicated his life and death to the poorest of men without help from God. The walls of the student halls of the world were chalked with the words, CHE LIVES. His martyrdom has been the condition for his inspiration of many of the young. He may have died for the poor, but he also died for posterity.

More immediately, Che's death coincided with the full fury of the Red Guard movement in Mao's China. With Che as their personal symbol and the Red Guards as their general model, many of the students of the world revolted in 1968. The events of that year were curiously similar to those of 1848, when a wave of insurrection had swept through most of the capital cities of Europe and had ended in the victory of the powers that were. The chief difference between the student revolts of 1968 and the middle-class revolts of 1848 lay in the shape of the new inspiration. For both Che and the Red Guards were inspired by the concept of a rural revolt that would sweep out of the countryside to purge the corruption of the cities. The middle-class students, who fought in the streets of Paris during the May Revolution, or of Chicago during the Democratic Convention, or of Berlin or London or Buenos Aires or Tokyo or Mexico City or twenty other cities during the year after Che's death, came from an urban or suburban setting. They did not want to know of their misconception of Che's and Mao's thought. Yet Mao was to remind them, when he sent off twenty million of the Red Guards back to labour in the countryside. As the *New China Daily* told the parents of Chinese youth, "The greatest love one can give one's sons and daughters is to encourage them to go to the front line of production and to temper themselves in the countryside ... through re-education by the poor peasants." Up to forty million people were to die in this re-education.

The governments of the world won in 1968. In Latin America, nearly all the guerrilla risings were suppressed. In Communist and capitalist countries, the protest of the young was defeated by the power of the old. Harsher measures were taken in Kenya as well as in Czechoslovakia, in Mexico as well as in France, in China as well as in the United States. This was a global reaction against a global revolt, partially inspired by Che's death. But just as Bolívar failed five times before succeeding in Latin America, and Che himself failed three times in Guatemala and the Congo and Bolivia for his one success in Cuba, so the failure of the revolts of 1968 did not mean the end of revolts. For Che's most explosive idea was that the revolution is permanent and that it creates itself. Authority has not sat safe in its seats, since that heresy reached the minds of the young.

Che's last rebellion was the spark to many fuses. In the United States, the phenomenon of the Hippies coincided with the disastrous war in Vietnam. The underground magazine *Open City* announced a VD or Vietnam Day, when tens of thousand of Hippies were called to disrupt an appearance by President Lyndon Johnson in Los Angeles, not with the usual cries of "Hey, Hey, LBJ, How Many Kids Did You Kill Today?," but with positive peace signs such as 'Welcome Hanoi to the Great Society'. It was time for aesthetic rebellion, for creative anarchy. "We must realise that numbers and time are on our side and that the Establishment needs us to fight this non-existent war ... Hippies of the world unite; you have nothing to lose but your paranoia."

Seeking Hippie support against Vietnam and racism were the organizing abilities of the Students for Democratic Society, led by the charismatic Tom Hayden, later the husband of Jane Fonda, who would be doomed to join rather than radicalize Hollywood. Hayden drafted the Port Huron statement of the movement; it tried to create a socialist student power on the back of the Free Speech turmoils at Berkeley, which culminated in a sit-in round the US Navy's recruitment table on campus in December, 1966, and intervention by the police. This was a declaration of independence of a new American revolution: "We, the people ..." became "We are the people of this generation, bred in at least modest comfort, housed now in universities, looking uncomfortably at the world we inherit. As we grew, however, our comfort was penetrated by events too troubling to dismiss. First, the permeating and victimising fear of human degradation, symbolised by the Southern struggle against racial bigotry, compelled most of us from silence to activism. Secondly, the enclosing fact of the Cold War, symbolised by the presence of the Bomb, brought awareness that we ourselves, and our friends, and millions ... might die at any time. We might deliberately ignore, or avoid, or fail to feel all other human problems, but not these two, for these were too immediate and crushing in their impact."

The Black Power movement was already refusing all help from whites and turning from the politics of integration towards revolution. It was the same with women activists, now more concerned with their own rights than those of oppressed blacks or colonial people. It would also be the turn of the gay movements, which would come out of the closet door, kicked open by the Hippie emphasis on open sexuality.

Yet the anarchist entry into political protest through the Yippies was to create a good deal of sound and fury, signifying not very much. Those who could organize protest, chiefly the apostles of student power and Black Power, discovered that an association with a permissive or a drug culture did their hard causes little good. Vietnam was the only banner to wave that could unite all those who might be drafted, but burning the American flag was not a recruiting card.

Two methods were being advocated of unseating governments – by outrage and fun, or by sabotage and gun. The Situationists and the Yippies supported revolution by spectacle, while the black and student power movements preferred guerrilla war. The Situationist revolution was through psychological and cultural overthrow rather than by street or factory violence. The radical poet Alexander Trocchi put its aims in subverting the whole world more emphatically than its leader Guy Debord did. The attack had to be cultural. With his thousand technicians, Trotsky had seized the bridges, telephone exchanges and the power stations. The police had guarded the government in the Kremlin, effectively blocking it from the real levers of power. "So the cultural revolt must seize the grids of expression and the powerhouses of the mind." Intelligence had to realize its own power on the global scale. Traditional authorities would be outflanked. What had to be seized had no physical dimensions. "It's not an arsenal, not a capital city, not an island, nor an isthmus visible from a peak in Darien." It was these things too, but only by the way, and inevitably "we must seize ourselves, the creative people, the millions of potential technicians." There was no permanence in human institutions or nature. "There is only becoming." By modifying, correcting, polluting, deflecting, corrupting, eroding and outflanking, what could be inspired was the invisible insurrection.

That insurrection had become visible at the University of Strasbourg in 1966, when some of the young Situationists followed Debord's tactics, expounded in his *The Society of the Spectacle*. They took over and bankrupted the student union there by printing a pamphlet on *The Poverty of Student Life*, claiming that art was dead, while the student was a necrophiliac and a conspicuous consumer. This example of subversion by the economic means of capitalism itself would be a path-finder for the revolt in Paris two years later, when Debord would find himself briefly in charge at the Sorbonne, before losing his power through ignorance about how to exercise it. No Trotsky he, and certainly no Lenin.

Such spectacles of the absurdity and contradictions of capitalism would also be played out at the Democratic Convention in Chicago by the American Yippies, but they seemed equally futile and contradictory to the leaders of the black and student power activists. The moderate and charismatic Martin Luther King finally had turned against the Vietnam War as a killing ground for blacks, and he had described the American government as "the greatest purveyor of violence in the world today." The Black Panthers, in their dark berets and glasses and leather, were armed and rising in the ghettos of Oakland across the Bay Bridge from San Francisco. The words of Stokely Carmichael and Huey Newton and Eldridge Cleaver and H. Rap Brown were widely reported and feared, particularly the notorious phrase that 'violence is as American as apple pie.'

The opening of the Free School in New York, where courses were offered on Mao and Black Power and 'Latin America – the next Vietnams?' was showing how the winds of radical change were beginning to blow across the campus and the university yard. The powers that were became frightened. On police evidence, Huey Newton was put in jail, as was Eldridge Cleaver for the second time, although it prompted the publication of his *Soul on Ice*, which seemed to favour the rape of white culture and a coalition with white radicalism in opposition to the separatist Black Power advocated by Stokely Carmichael. As if to shroud the growing miasma of violence, a new series of killings of great men thwarted history. Andy Warhol's cliché about everybody being a celebrity for a quarter of an hour held a grain of missing truth, especially for murderers.

In point of fact, we are all intermittently a part of history, when we feel ourselves to be involved. Particularly, the slaughter of our heroes can provoke street and private rebellions, and for seconds or hours, for days or weeks, we may threaten the security of governments. In Bolivia the army, helped by American CIA agents and detector helicopters, killed Che Guevara. In certain radical circles, it was equivalent to the killing of Christ, and the iconography of the posters of the student world treated Che's death in that way. His beret as a halo round his head, his beard as an aureole, sometimes clutching the rifle of revolution in his hand, Che's martyred countenance was displayed on the walls of a million university rooms. Although the authorities required his body to be burned and his ashes scattered so that there could be no shrine to him, his two forearms were severed and these holy relics of the liberation struggle were eventually smuggled back to Havana.

Cuba had become the darling of the new Left, an island that could cock a snook, if not a missile, at the almighty Uncle Sam only a hundred sea miles away. There lay the model contemporary revolution, where a small band of guerrillas operating from the countryside had destroyed an urban dictator in Havana and had brought equality and literacy to an oppressed people. The tens of thousands of political prisoners, held by Castro and his ubiquitous informers on every block and in each village, were as invisible to the foreign radicals as the Gulag had been to the fellow-travellers in Stalin's heyday.

The Havana Cultural Congress in the January of 1968 attracted nearly four hundred intellectuals from Latin and North America and Europe. Many of them were members of the Fair Play for Cuba Committee, which had been formed eight years previously, and which boasted leading authorities such as Sartre with his strident and blinkered anti-Americanism and C. Wright Mills, who put aside his examination of *The Power Elite* to tell his country to 'Listen, Yankee' and follow the Cuban path in emancipating blacks and women and poor agricultural workers. A feeling of hope and urgency in changing human society as well as the possibility of doing it was a potent brew for the new radicals – even more exciting than John F. Kennedy's inauguration had been for a previous generation. The rhetoric seemed much the same, although the disaster of the invasion at the Bay of Pigs and the continuing American blockade still lay between the two countries. Ask not what Cuba can do for you, ask what you can do for Cuba.

The bad temper of the times was high on sporadic violence and low on an agreed ideology. The further killings of Robert Kennedy and of Martin Luther King appeared to be the apogee of the reign of personal terror instead of political persuasion. The rules of the game were reversed. Bullets and not ballots, assassinations and not armies, were the preferred instruments of change. Paradoxically, the killing of the younger Kennedy, as he was running successfully for the White House in an effort to unseat Lyndon Johnson, defused the rising revolt against the Vietnamese War, particularly when Johnson himself refused to run again. The shooting down of both the Kennedy brothers showed that nobody was safer in Dallas or San Francisco than in Hanoi or Saigon.

When you met murder on the way, it did not wear the mask of LBJ, but that of an anonymous gunman, famous only for a brutal and almost pointless act – its only purpose to make a celebrity out of obscurity. What the leading American social historian Richard Hofstadter had found most despairing about his own society was its inability to come to terms with guns. They remained the 'equalizers' of a polyglot continental people, who were given unequal opportunities, yet were dedicated to the liberty to possess a weapon. "Guns are neat little things, aren't they?" the attempted assassin of the actor and future president, Ronald Reagan, would say. "They can kill extraordinary people with very little effort."

In an article on 'Assassination: The Ultimate Public Theatre', reprinted in the programme for Stephen Sondheim's brilliant and ineluctable musical *Assassins*, Robert Jay Lifton affirmed that the pistol or rifle was the appropriate technology "for annihilating king, leader and father, for becoming immortal by absorbing the power of all three. The 'equalizer' presides over a grotesque caricature of American Egalitarianism." An article of my own on the killing of great men noted the courage of ex-President Theodore Roosevelt in continuing a public speech, while pouring with blood after being shot in the heart and only saved by his spectacle-case. He reckoned that assassination was 'a trade risk, which every prominent public man ought to accept as a matter of course'. But it seemed a paradox to me, because political assassination was justified in a sense by its success.

The questions posed at the murder of Thomas à Becket or of Guevara have never been solved. Does the safety of the state demand that a rebel should be butchered in cold blood, even if he happens to be a brave man halfway to sainthood? And if that sort of state exists, capable of using murder as a weapon, then does not each man have the right to pick up a gun and assassinate the agents of the government in order to create a better one? In a police state which denies human rights, who is the political assassin – the tyrannical policeman who murders the innocent citizen, or the armed citizen who murders the soldier obeying orders? The answer is brutal in history. All assassinations which succeed in changing governments for long periods of time are accepted by their societies, and thus justified. All political assassinations which fail are condemned as treason. As in so many walks of life, in the murder of the great, success is justification.

The assassination of Martin Luther King in Memphis, however, was conspicuous by its failure. It killed the man, but it won his cause, which was delivered by the white murderer into the hands of the advocates of black power. There were riots in the ghettos of one hundred and ten American cities, the National Guard was called to quell the disturbances, and twenty-five hundred people were killed or injured. Yet this was not a political explosion, but an orgy of arson and looting and aimless counter-violence. It was not what the leaders of the Black Muslims and the Black Panthers had threatened, a race war in the streets unless all the demands for black emancipation and equality were immediately granted. It was the explosion of mass outrage at the death of a hero, who would later be doomed by the saliva of biographers to sexual innuendo and denigration, as the Kennedy brothers were to be. But at the time, he and the Kennedys had been the messengers of a new hope in a new society: no historical retrospective could change those facts. H. Rap Brown was wrong in hailing the widespread ghetto riots as 'a rehearsal for revolution', and Tom Hayden in seeing them as an American form of slum guerrilla warfare. They represented an enraged process of the deprived, laying hands on what they could get and destroying what they could not possess.

Driving to Paris in May, 1968, to rescue a revolutionary wife, Marianne, who compiled *Viva Che!*, I had four jerry-cans of petrol on my roof-rack because there were none to be had in France. On the roads outside the provincial towns, the gates of the factories were barred and red flags flew from the machine shops, while men stood idle, peering through the wire and the grilles at the future. They shouted 'profiteer' at me because of the cans of gasoline on the car roof. On television, Prime Minister Pompidou appeared beaten, giving huge concessions to the workers – more than nine of twenty million were on strike. President Charles de Gaulle had flown to Germany to check on the loyalty of the seventy thousand troops in the French Zone; their tanks were said to be rolling towards the embattled capital.

When I reached our apartment in Paris, Marianne was lost in the Sorbonne, so I went to the Theatre of the Revolution at l'Odéon, which had been taken over as a night-and-day debating chamber by the rebels. Drama had become real, the Marat/Sade play was a street event, the halls being made into parliaments. Stephen Spender was there, and he found it like the sixth act in a Theatre of Cruelty. Although the performances were chaotic, they seemed to the audience more entertaining than Ionesco or Beckett. Spender noted that the Paris students were like Hippies without a drug culture; they wished to live the life of the revolution even while they were taking action to bring it to be. They did not wish to hear of the downfall of the anarchists in the Spanish Republic, who had also wanted democracy.

La Jeunesse fait le P...

Their revolution was thought to be new and unprecedented. The others might have failed, but theirs would succeed. As three of their slogans went: I TAKE WHAT I WANT AS REALITY BECAUSE I BELIEVE IN THE REALITY OF WHAT I WANT, and: BE REALISTS, DEMAND THE IMPOSSIBLE, and: RUN, COMRADE, THE OLD WORLD IS BEHIND YOU.

Although I thought I knew that the failure of the student revolt was certain, there was a contagion of hope at the barricaded Sorbonne, where more slogans were scrawled on the walls: HERE ALIENATION BEGINS – RATHER LIFE! and: YOUTH IS ETERNAL DRUNKENNESS, IT IS THE FEVER OF REASON, a phrase that Rimbaud could have written. Already new authoritarian groups were taking over from the free-style fighting students, hurling their cobblestones at the riot police, the fearsome CRS with black helmets and plastic shields. Ex-mercenaries from the troubles in Africa, the Katangais, were introducing the methods of their opponents into the revolutionary cause: extortion and beating and rape. As another graffito read: LIBERTY IS THE CRIME THAT CONTAINS ALL CRIMES. IT IS OUR ABSOLUTE WEAPON.

While the forces of repression and the state grouped for a showdown, the students seemed to shift from demands for reform to the desire for an apocalypse. Sinister scrawls on the walls such as: AND IF WE BURNED THE SORBONNE? caused a shift of Parisian feeling from favouring the rebel cause to vilifying it. Too many cars had been torched or made into barricades, private property was under threat. Noam Chomsky had told the occupation squads at Columbia University in New York that they would rather Karl Marx had burned down the British Museum than worked on *Das Kapital* in it, and Stephen Spender echoed the thoughts, coming to the conclusion that however much the university needed a revolution, and their society needed a revolution, these were separate issues for the Sorbonne activists, who might still use the weapons of the trained mind. "For the university, even if it does not conform to their wishes, is an arsenal from which they can draw the arms which can change society."

Marianne, too, saw the change in conditions in the Sorbonne, although she would not come back with me to England. She would fight on to the bitter end. Her worst experience had been when she was swept to the front of a mob trying to storm the Senate. Two iron barriers secured by a chain held back the press, and through the chink between them, she saw machine-gunners waiting behind their weapons for the charge and the inevitable massacre. But government agent *déprovocateurs* dressed in students' clothing had shouted to the crowd to attack another government target, the *doppelgängers* of Dany Cohn-Bendit, who had started the whole revolt in the concrete jungle of isolated Nanterre, one of the new French universities so similar to the concrete ziggurats of those being built in England.

Marianne also saw the writing on the wall, with the reaction of the right wing to de Gaulle's deal with the Communists, who hated this explosion of anarchism and radicalism outside their Stalinist control of the faithful in France. The President promised general elections and gave the unions great concessions, their leaders could return to the workers with more wages and less factory hours, the students were now isolated. The Champs Élysées was packed with the cars of the bourgeoisie hooting the five-note slogan, 'Al-gé-rie Fran-çaise', for the Algerian war had divided French society as the Vietnam one had America. It was 'the triumphant bacchanal of the Social World of Conspicuous Consumption, shameless, crowing, and more vulgar' than any crowd that Spender had ever seen on Broadway or in Chicago.

For it was the consumer and manipulative society that the revolt had attacked – and the workers and their leaders had now sold out and adopted it. Most of the slogans on the walls bore the same message:

> THE MORE YOU CONSUME, THE LESS YOU LIVE
> SOCIETY IS A CARNIVOROUS FLOWER
> MAN MAKES LOVE WITH THINGS
> MERCHANDISE IS THE OPIUM OF THE PEOPLE
> HIDE YOURSELF, OBJECT!
> HAPPINESS IS BOUGHT – STEAL IT
> THE IMAGINATION TO POWER
> DOWN WITH ACCOUNTS, LONG LIVE THE EPHEMERAL
> UNIONS ARE BROTHELS
> NO BARRACKS FOR THE SPIRIT
> ART IS DEAD – DO NOT EAT ITS CORPSE
> CULTURE IS THE INVERSION OF LIFE
> DON'T CHANGE MASTERS, BECOME THE MASTER OF YOUR LIFE
> NO MORE, GRAND PATRON!

And on one of the dozens of street posters manufactured at the occupied École des Beaux Arts, a radical conjugation:

> I PARTICIPATE
> YOU PARTICIPATE
> HE PARTICIPATES
> WE PARTICIPATE
> YOU PARTICIPATE
> THEY PROFIT

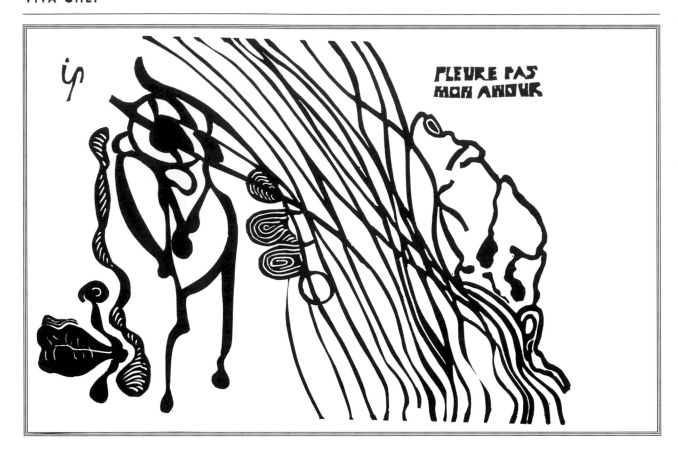

French Revolutionary Poster, 1968.

The Beaux Arts was almost the last of the occupied buildings to fall, and under attack, Marianne was given the original of its most famous poster to take away to safety, the blue-black shape of a riot policeman looking like a space terminator with his truncheon raised, and CRS = SS blazoned on his shield. She gave it to me to carry away to England to commemorate the failing rebellion, along with two other significant posters, one of de Gaulle's shadow holding a hand over a young man's mouth: BE YOUNG AND SHUT UP, and the other of the radicals' defiance of anodyne democracy, de Gaulle hitting France with a tricoloured baton and saying: KEEP VOTING – I'LL DO THE REST.

As I left Paris for Calais and the ferry, I picked up three battered students from Rouen and Boulogne, who had come into the capital to protest, and now were going home, because they were frightened and beaten. They were very young and had no ideology; they had joined in the struggle for the excitement and for the attack on all authority, particularly their *lycées* and their parents and the dreaded *bac*, the universal examination. If there was any slogan that took their fancy, it was: THE MORE I MAKE LOVE, THE MORE I WANT TO MAKE A REVOLUTION. THE MORE I WANT TO MAKE A REVOLUTION, THE MORE I WANT TO MAKE LOVE.

The defeat of the students in Paris did not lose their war across the world, although it was an unsettling example, as the defeat of the Commune had been in 1848, when most of the cities of Europe had exploded in rebellion before they were repressed. A map of contemporary outbreaks of urban violence printed in *L'Événement* with its graffito on the cover; WHY IT ISN'T FINISHED YET, showed six revolts in Japan, one in South Korea, one each in Indonesia and Malaya, regular uprisings in China, two outbursts in India, five in the Middle East and another five in Africa, five again in eastern Europe and five in Italy, many in Germany where the Berlin student leader Rudi Deutschke had been shot in the head, some in Spain and the Low Countries and Scandinavia and Britain, eleven in South America and two only in the United States. The example of Paris, however, had ignited the students of the globe, who had nothing to lose but their final examinations. Massively repressed in every country, the scattered fires still spluttered in England, as always a little behind the times and never knowing when it was beaten.

The analysis of why the students had lost was already under way in France, where the intellectuals such as Sartre would always rather diagnose a failure than support a fragmented rebellion. He had begun by praising the young, saying, "Your movement is interesting because it puts imagination in power." Something which astonished, something which jolted, something which repudiated all that had made French society what it was then, had come out of the revolt. But it could not work, because anarchists and fragmentary Trotskyite groups could not organize the masses of the workers. The rebellion could only pave the way with cobblestones for the Marxist revolution and the dictatorship of the proletariat, which was not yet ready to happen. There was no chance of Dany Cohn-Bendit's vision of a federation of workers' councils and soviets and strikers running the country in a classless society. The angry older men, indeed, such as John Osborne, vehemently repudiated such a vision, saying to Ken Tynan: "Student power is a very factitious thing. It always seems to me that, 'What am I?' is a much more interesting question than, 'What are we?' ... What happened at the Sorbonne seemed more animal than human to me ... The prospect of rule by instant rabble doesn't appeal to me either."

The failure of the urban revolts led by students referred the attention of the new Left to the example of Mao and Castro and Che and the Vietcong. Régis Debray, put in prison for a while during Guevara's campaign in Bolivia, but soon released, had come out in 1967 in his *Revolution within the Revolution?* with the *foco* theory, using Cuba particularly as an example. The establishment and uninterrupted development of a guerrilla nucleus in the countryside was the key to the revolutionary process. First, it attracted peasants to the cause; secondly, it defeated scattered government forces; thirdly, it drew support from the towns; finally, it took over the capital by infiltration as well as attack. The book was written before Guevara's disastrous attempt to create a *foco* in Bolivia, but the successful Cuban example under Castro and the struggle of the Vietcong from the jungle toward Saigon were magnets for those radical activists, moving more and more towards guerrilla acts of sporadic violence from motivated cells or *groupuscules*, set against the power of the capitalist state.

For, as in Hungary at the time of Suez, which had started my own personal rebellion, Russia again was forfeiting all pretence to be the backer of socialist revolutions across the world by intervening in Czechoslovakia to conserve its eastern European empire. The Prague Spring had been the only successful urban revolution in 1968, but the rise of the Dubcek régime to power was a middle-class uprising of the intelligentsia, resenting Soviet and socialist control over economic activity and political life. At the end of August, a quarter of a million troops crossed the frontiers to crush the reforms. Russian tanks surrounded Wenceslas Square and united the Czech nation by their act of aggression.

Although the Czech leadership was summoned to Moscow and bullied into submission, Soviet power was revealed as a gun barrel behind a brazen mask. Two thousand workers at the CKD factory in Prague described the Russia of Chairman Brezhnev as it was, 'an imperialist state with all its characteristic attributes ... neither the homeland of socialism nor a shield of socialism.' The Tsars had put out the last lights of rebellion in 1848, and now, one hundred and twenty years later, that final extinction was the act of a Politburo in the Kremlin. Refusing to adapt, the Communist leaders doomed the Union of Soviet Socialist Republics to future disintegration.

Lyndon Johnson had already dug the grave of his political career during the Vietnamese War, while his refusal to run again led to the Democratic Convention ending in sad farce and despair rather than street drama and hope. His fall and the preoccupation of most of the western nations with their own domestic riots had made Brezhnev feel secure enough to invade Czechoslovakia, just as the involvement of the West in the Suez affair had permitted the Hungarian invasion. But the foregone conclusion of the Democratic Convention – the nomination of the good grey man of liberal reform politics, Hubert Humphrey, against the ex-member of the House Un-American Activities Committee and backer of Senator McCarthy, Richard Nixon, vitiated the plans to disrupt it. Uselessly, Tom Hayden tried to set up a socialist and anti-imperialist demonstration against a party leader, clean of policy in Vietnam and preferable to the tricky Republican candidate, who had made his name in a crusade against reds under the beds. To the Cuban Revolution, he was merely another badmouth with fangs.

So the power of protest was delivered to the Yippies, led by Jerry Rubin, once a leader of the Free Speech Movement in Berkeley, who defined his strategy and tactics as 'happenings, community, youth power, dignity, underground media, music, legends, marijuana, action, myth, excitement, a new style.' Another bright light among the Yippies was Abbie Hoffman, who had left the civil rights movement for the alternative culture, claiming that 'long hair makes us the new niggers,' as a symbol of rejection of the old order. The Chicago police and the National Guard were mobilized by the tough and reactionary Mayor Daley to see that the Democratic Convention was not disrupted by the tens of thousands of drop-outs and several hundred radicals, who gathered in Grant Park to hear the rants of their leaders and of some of the greater rebels of western literature, Burroughs and Genet and Mailer. The clashes between the police, supported by the guardsmen and the Yippie rioters in the park and later in Michigan Avenue, were more violent than those in Paris, the clubbings and the tear gas, the curses and the stomping. Even the convention delegates and the news commentators were beaten.

The only black elected to the Georgia State Legislature, Julian Bond, said in a speech that he had never seen the police behave with more brutality in Mississippi or Alabama or his own state. Unfortunately, the mass of the American people approved of this assault on the long-haired and wayward 'children' of the new age: their antics were orgies that provoked violence, their picnics in the park were plots to subvert the American way of life – they were, indeed, in the Yippie manifesto, which called for the legalization of all psychedelic drugs, the abolition of all laws relating to crimes without victims, the total disarmament of all the people beginning with the police, the abolition of money, full unemployment and fucking anywhere, anyone at any time.

There was no dialogue between the radicals and the liberals, Trotskyites and Maoists, young and old, or black and white. And much worse was the gap between rhetoric and reality. The Black Panthers, now led by Eldridge Cleaver, wanted guns and a war of liberation before there was genocide. But few of the radicals thought a revolution was possible, while the Left was so divided and isolated from the rest of the community. They were split, anyway, between those who believed in organization and those who trusted in spontaneity. The first group wanted limited action, the second daring protests that might spark off wider action, as at Prague and in Paris. But no reliance could be placed on the 'masses' to support a revolution, as they were mainly getting what they wanted from the system.

These ripples of spontaneous action did widen to some of the British universities, particularly the newer ones. Although there had been turmoils at the London School of Economics two years previously and also at the Regent Street Polytechnic and the Holborn College of Law and Commerce in the capital, the contagion of student revolt, demanding representation on governing bodies, spread to Birmingham and Leicester and Hull and chiefly to Essex, the new university where I had been offered the Department of American Studies. There, a strike supporting three suspended students and demands for places in the Senate led to the founding of an alternative university on the site and to Situationist pranks against the authorities. Had I been teaching there, I would have probably followed the reaction of most of the other professors, an initial sympathy with the wishes of the students, ending in anger at disruptive tactics that effectively put an end to the possibility of education or examination. The problem of a 'free' university was that every undergraduate was free to learn nothing much and occupy a place. Personal liberty would mean a deliberate choice of continuing ignorance. As the Chairman of the Board of Governors, Lord Robbins, declared after another student occupation of the London School of Economics, "You can't have a democracy paying the money for youngsters to do what they like."

For the first time since the General Strike, the authorities in London feared an insurrection in the capital, when the Vietnam Solidarity Campaign announced another march on the American Embassy in Grosvenor Square. Previous marches had led to running battles between demonstrators and mounted policemen, and to scenes of violence in the green garden of the square that could have been played on the Boulevard Saint-Germain or Michigan Avenue. *The Times* lost its nerve, claimed there was a plot to seize vital installations and television stations, and advised all major offices and shops to put up steel shutters for the day. Reduced to watching rather than participating, I joined the American author Mary McCarthy as an observer for the National Council for Civil Liberties on that day of conflict, in which the divided radicals and splintered Left threw away any chance of changing British politics by defiance in the streets.

The anarchists and Maoists and Stalinists wanted a direct attack on the American embassy, but the main organizers of the march, Tariq Ali and his helpers on the Trotskyite radical magazine *The Black Dwarf*, decided to avoid a confrontation and march their hundred thousand supporters to Hyde Park for peaceful dispersal. "This was the largest explicitly revolutionary demonstration since the 'twenties," Ali wrote in his autobiography, *Street Fighting Years*. "We were not crazed utopians and the ruling classes in Western Europe did not see us as such, but as the advance guard of a new order. We wished to transform Western civilization because we regarded it as politically, morally and culturally bankrupt."

Whatever his beliefs and strategy, Tariq Ali and his organizers acted out the role of the agents *déprovocateurs*, who had turned Marianne and the Paris mob away from the machine-gunners outside the French Senate. Bullhorns and megaphones persuaded the vast majority of the marchers to progress peacefully to disintegration in Hyde Park. Mary McCarthy and I watched a few thousand anarchists and Maoists attack the American Embassy and Ten Downing Street. On the last of the Aldermaston marches, I had fought along with the anarchists and run with their red-and-black flag past the Houses of Parliament. Now I stood on the sidelines, watching the police horses stamp the assault on the embassy to bruises and later break up the anarchists in the Mall as they chanted, "Wilson, we want you dead!" The whole mass protest seemed as futile and temporary as an electric storm, all that rage and fizzing and dislocated howling, achieving nothing.

After the failure of the student risings of 1968, the political rebels took two opposed paths – either into extreme violence or into compromise and inclusion. It was the same for popular music in that last year of the decade, the ultimate communion of mass love preached by the Beatles at Woodstock, set against the aggression chanted by the Rolling Stones at Altamont. Urban guerrilla factions were starting to split from the radical student bodies, the Weathermen and the Revolutionary Youth Movement in America, the Red Brigades in Italy, the Red Army Faction or Baader-Meinhof gang in Germany, the Angry Brigade in Britain, and Action Directe in France. They supported John Lee Hooker singing 'Motor City is Burning': "all the cities will burn . . . you are the people who will build up the ashes." The Black Panthers were descending into paranoia and criminal acts. Eldridge Cleaver and other Panthers broke parole and jail, hijacking aircraft and descending on Cuba, the last hope of the revolutionaries. They had not won the backing of the black ghettos, terrified at their tactics of armed confrontation. "We thought of ourselves as a vanguard," Huey Newton was soon to confess. "When we looked around we found we were not the vanguard for anything, we lost the favour of the black community and left it behind."

The same collapse was evident in the disintegration of pop art. Even *Oz*, in a bitter article on the Institute of Contemporary Arts in London, 'Ho! Ho! Ho Chi Mall', accused it of being the worst and most insecure part of the old Arts Establishment and cashing in on the doomed 'revolutionary rave-up'. Che Guevara and Paris and the occupation of the Hornsey College of Art had all occurred on cue, "just as flower power began wilting, to give the same old magazines another set of slogans, of innovations, of trends ... Increasingly the attack on art is also an attack on integrity in the name of the mass produced, easily consumed, throwaway, knick-knack objects. Consume

faster! consume everything! don't think about anything! Buy art! Buy art's art! Buy non-art! You too can be a collector!" The revolutionary posters from the Beaux Arts were already hot collectors' items. "Buy a History of Anti-Art! Buy an Anti-History of Anti-Art! Buy the Anti-Art Bulletin! Objects! Institutes! New! Revolutionary! Happenings!"

This disillusion with the consumption and decline of the alternative culture along with student and black protest in the Old World did not extend to the Third World. The hope of those who still could hope for political change no longer lay in the *foco* or urban guerrilla resistance in the major capitalist cities, although the Weathermen bombarded seven major companies in New York in a year, causing more than forty deaths and twenty million dollars' worth of damage. The last hopes lay in Cuba and in Vietnam. These were the chief combatants against the evils of imperialism, which had now become the rallying cry among all other cries as it had been in the 'thirties, now that the majority of student and black activists were moving towards an accommodation with the powers that were in their own countries.

Che Guevara was the apostle and the martyr of this last hope. As John Berger wrote in an article for Marianne's illustrated *Viva Che*, the photograph of his corpse reminded him of Mantegna's painting of the dead Christ that now hangs in the Brera at Milan. "Guevara was no Christ. If I see the Mantegna again in Milan, I shall see in it the body of Guevara. But this is only because in certain rare cases the tragedy of a man's death completes and exemplifies the meaning of his whole life. I am acutely aware of that about Guevara, and certain painters were once aware of it about Christ." Guevara had found the condition of the world intolerable. Imperialism had demanded cheap raw materials, exploited labour and a controlled world market. Now it demanded a mankind that counted for nothing. Guevara had foreseen his own end in the revolutionary fight against this imperialism. At the news of his death, Berger had heard somebody say, " 'He was the world symbol of the possibilities of one man.' Why was this true? Because he recognized what was intolerable for man and acted accordingly."

Although I did not believe that Che's example could succeed outside Latin America – and so I wrote in a short book on Guevara for the *Modern Masters Series*, which included Fanon along with Wittgenstein, and McLuhan along with Trotsky, as the teachers of our time – I was an admirer of his asthmatic courage in taking to the jungle to capture a continent, the ultimate in reckless commitment. When Marianne brought to me from the Cuban embassy in London his authentic *Bolivian Diary*, not the *ersatz* CIA version published elsewhere, I was moved enough to translate it with an exiled Argentinian student and to publish it. The secret services of four countries now put us under surveillance: those of America and Britain, France and Cuba. It was, however, invaluable in gaining me a Cuban visa, when I had to go there in 1969 to extricate Marianne from her revolutionary folly.

The style of the *Bolivian Diary* then seemed to me as flat and necessary as that of Robinson Crusoe, yet its cumulative effect was even more powerful and moving than Defoe's masterpiece, because the reader knew in advance that the hero would be captured and executed, when the pages of the diary went blank. I wrote of the *Bolivian Diary*:

At the beginning, the war games of the guerrilla seem no more real than Boy Scouts at play; then real deaths begin, in torrents or in ambush. Bitter quarrels break out over a tin of condensed milk. All of living is stripped to the essence of survival, dominated only by the commitment of Guevara and his men. There is no need to talk of the reality of the book, for it is real. And the sparseness of its prose contains the dignity, humanity, and spirit of the only Garibaldi of our age. It is sad that our country, which took Garibaldi to its heart because then it backed the revolution of its time – the liberal and national revolution – should now react to Guevara with fear because he has tried to be the new Bolívar and unite Latin America in one whole against poverty and oppression. The Old World has, indeed, aged when it cannot appreciate the hope of the New.

My hopes for a radical change of the world ended in a personal black comedy. Heavily pregnant, Marianne had run off to her beloved Cuba. She intended to present her child to the revolution there; but she lost her nerve after eight months of waiting around in Havana. We were in trouble, because of Marianne's close friendship with Eldridge Cleaver and other Black Panthers, who had hijacked American aeroplanes to join Castro. They intended, as latterday Che Guevaras, to invade Mississippi, armed to the teeth, in a dinghy. So the six of them would liberate the slave South. They would even fight the Cuban army, for what they perceived as its oppression of many black countrymen.

News of our preparations for armed resistance; a personal letter from Cleaver to Castro, carried by Marianne; the fact that we were more trouble than we were worth; the fear by Castro of provoking another Bay of Pigs if the Panthers were allowed to invade America in their rubber boat; the damage to the Cuban image if a few foreigners were eliminated in a fire-fight: all or none of these led to a drama that ended not in a bang, but in a damp squib. Our passports were restored to us. Places were found on the Cuban airline to Madrid for Marianne and myself, although she was only a couple of weeks from giving birth. The Panthers were booked to Algeria, which had agreed to take them in, rather too far away for them to mount any invasion of the United States overnight.

Before our permitted flight, I affirmed that we would continue the Revolution in our own countries. My publishing company would print the trials of Fidel Castro and Régis Debray and a book against the American war in Vietnam. And Marianne's revolutionary fervour did not abate: a few weeks after the birth of her boy, she would leave for Pyongyang in North Korea and demonstrate on the edge of the demilitarised Zone with Cleaver against the American troops standing with the South Koreans on the far side. We kept our bargains. My small experience with secret policemen is that they do not do you in, as long as you refuse to take their money, and do what you say.

As with all cultural history, we may only record our personal involvement and sentiment, although I was present at many of the greater occasions of Che's early influence on events in Cuba and Paris, London and Chicago. He was the ikon of the radical age at the end of the nineteen-sixties. The rising rebels found it easy to identify with Che. What he did and tried to do made the impossible for them appear to be possible. He was not a product of historical necessity. He was a revolutionary who chose to be so. Thus his example gave hope to all those, such as Régis Debray, who wished to work for the poor and the lost of the world without having been born black or oppressed or underprivileged. Birth did not make Che. He was self-made.

No other revolutionary hero will supplant Che. The rapid development of his cult after his death was the logical outcome of the end of his life, which had been spent in an atmosphere of secrecy, mystery, potency, and combat. Che's cowardly murder brought him instant consecration, because his death made certain all the qualities ascribed to him. His choice to leave Cuba and his martyrdom for his cause set him above Fidel Castro or Ho Chi Minh or Mao Tse-tung as a symbol of revolution, even though his talents as a guerrilla leader may have been inferior.

If Che had remained in Cuba or had died accidentally as Camilo Cienfuegos, his portrait would not have been paraded by students all over the world, his example would not have been quoted everywhere, his works would not have been so widely read. Not only Marxists, but almost all progressives, and even pacifists who qualified their admiration for Che by warning that they disagreed with some of his methods, would agree with Fidel's praise of Che's qualities as a man: "If we wish to express what we want the men of future generations to be, we must say: Let them be like Che".

In every cult, there is an element of the untrue and the irrational. In the cult of Che, that element was his identification with Christ. Because he fought for the poor and because he chose to be sacrificed in his prime, he gave a mystical feeling that he died for us, for all humanity. Clearly, he killed other men. Clearly, he hated his enemies. Clearly, his beliefs stemmed from political doctrines loathsome to many. Clearly, he advocated and used tactics that were sometimes dubious or inhuman. Clearly, he was a man who lived in his muck and sweat like a beast in the jungle. Yet clearly, he transcended all these facts.

He appeared as larger than a human being, as somebody approaching a saviour. When all is said and done, when his words and acts have been coldly seen and sometimes condemned, the conviction remains that Che was always driven by his love for humanity and for the good in mankind. The ideals expressed in his writings, his whole life and his passion and his death, bypassed ideology. The photograph of his corpse was pinned as an icon in many country homes across Catholic Latin America.

Sartre was correct when he called Che "the most complete man of his age." There was a Renaissance quality about Che; he had more careers in thirty-nine years than a whole squad of men have in their lives, and he had more lives than any litter of cats. He tried to be professional in everything he did, as a doctor, a diarist, a political and military theorist, a guerrilla fighter, an economist, a tactician, a banker, a planner, an industrialist, an ambassador, a propagandist, and as the doer of all his other duties. But he was complete in more than his work. He was all in one piece. He seems to have had hardly any contradictions or inner conflicts. He was amazingly consistent in all he said and thought and did. The professional administrator who discussed the economy of Latin America was no different from the guerrilla hero in Bolivia, who had decided that combat was the only way of solving his continent's social and economic problems. The difference between Che and other men was that Che did not let other men put his ideas into practice. He practised them himself.

There was no duality between Che's actions and his words. The writer practised what he preached and put other intellectuals to shame. The man of action set down his experiences and analyzed them to draw practical and moral conclusions from them. The dreamer applied his skills in trying to make his dreams concrete. Che was an absolutist. He wanted to pursue everything to its just conclusion. His consistency was almost maddening in its effortlessness. There was no trace of hypocrisy in him. When he said that working for one's fellow men was the greatest joy a man could have, it was true for him. He thought it was fit for a revolutionary to go and die under the flag of a nation not yet born, and he did just that, not making a great display of courage, but being courageous and cheerful as if he were doing the most natural thing in all the world. He said that no one was irreplaceable and really felt that this applied to him as much as to anyone else. So he exposed himself and died. He was a complete man.

History will probably treat Guevara as the Garibaldi of his age, the most admired and loved revolutionary of his time. The impact of his

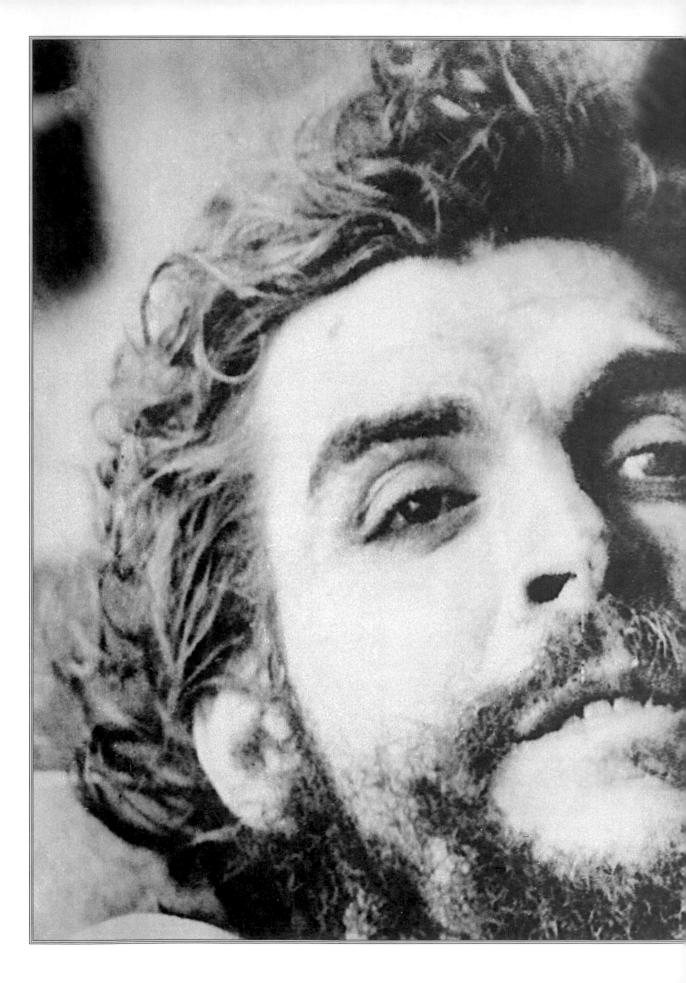

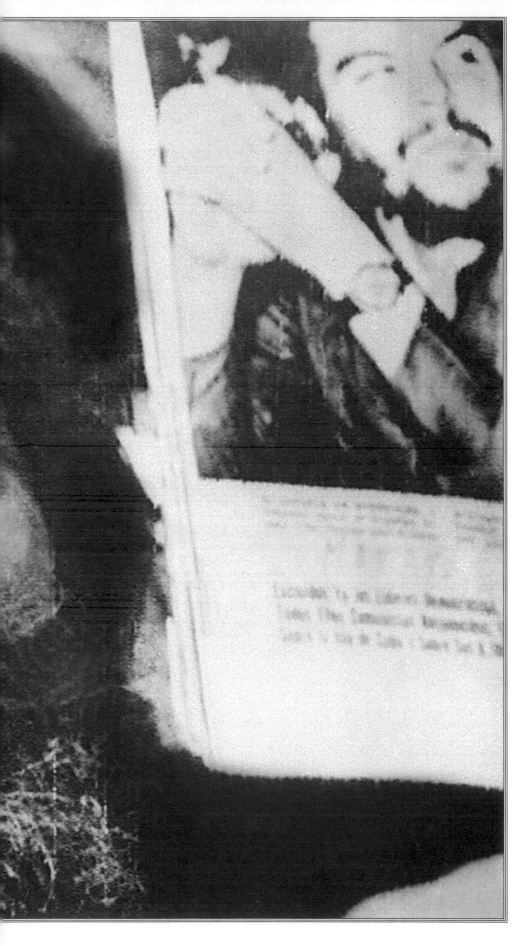

A close-up of the dead Che Guevara. A photograph of him alive has been placed next to him for identification.

ideas on socialism and guerrilla warfare may be temporary; but his influence, particularly in Latin America, must be lasting. For since Bolívar, there has been no man with so great an ideal of unity for that divided and unlucky continent. The young will find new heroes, but none more inspiring. And the consequences of his death are still to be seen in the social upheavals and changes around us. When the general in *Viva Zapata!* looks down at the riddled corpse of the dead guerrilla leader, he says, "Sometimes a dead man can be a terrible enemy." For the rich nations of the earth, and for the corrupt governments that rule many of the poor nations, the dead Che is a terrible and a beautiful enemy.

ANDREW SINCLAIR

Index

Page numbers in italics refer to illustrations in the text and those in bold to the plates.